Norman doorway at Ewhurst

GW00499508

THE OLD
PARISH CHURCHES
OF SURREY

Mike Salter

FOLLY PUBLICATIONS

Peter Newsman · Nov. 28th '00

ACKNOWLEDGEMENTS

The photographs in this book were taken by the author, who also drew the map, and the plans and sketches. Brass rubbings and old postcards are reproduced from the author's collections. The author would like to thank Kerin Fogerty for assistance with transport and accommodation during fieldwork for this book in 1999.

ABOUT THIS BOOK

As with the other churches books in this series (see full list inside back cover) this book concentrates on the period before the Industrial Revolution of the late 18th century and the subsequent dramatic population increases in London and the Home Counties necessitated the construction of a fresh series of new churches to serve the expanding urban areas. Most furnishings and monuments after 1800 are not mentioned in this book, although additions and alterations to older churches are. Churches founded after 1800 are not mentioned in the gazetteers, except in a few cases where new churches superseded older ones on different sites, but post-1800 churches are listed with some brief details separately at the back of the book.

This book includes the former Middlesex urban districts of Staines and Sunbury, joined to Surrey in 1965, and also the boroughs of Croydon, Kingston, Merton, Richmond and Sutton, once part of Surrey but since 1965 part of Greater London.

This book is inevitably very much a catalogue of descriptions, dates and names. It is intended as a field guide and for reference rather than to be read from cover to cover. Sometimes there are comments about the settings of churches but on the whole lack of space permits few comments about their position or atmosphere. Occasionally the most interesting features of a church or graveyard may lie outside the scope of this book as outlined above. The gazetteer features Ordnance Survey grid references (these are the two letters and six digits which appear after each place-name and dedication) and is intended to be used in conjunction with O.S. 1:50,000 scale maps. These are vital for finding the right church amongst the urban sprawl.

Plans redrawn from the author's field notes are reproduced to a common scale of 1:400. The building were measured in metres and only metric scales are given. For those who feel a need to convert three metres is almost ten feet. A system of hatching common to all the church plans in the books in this series is used to denote the different periods of work. On some pages there may be insufficient space for a key to the hatching to be shown. Where this is the case refer to another page. The plans should be treated with some caution. Some features are difficult to date and others are not easy to depict on small scale drawings, such as dressed (cut) stones of one period being reused in a later period, sometimes in a different place.

ABOUT THE AUTHOR

Mike Salter is 47 and has been a professional author-publisher since he went on the Government Enterprise Allowance Scheme for unemployed people in 1988. He is particularly interested in the planning and layout of medieval buildings and has a huge collection of plans of churches and castles he has measured during tours (mostly by bicycle and motorcycle) of all parts of the British Isles since 1968. Wolverhampton born and bred, Mike now lives in an old cottage beside the Malvern Hills. His other interests include walking, maps, railways, board games, morris dancing, playing percussion instruments and calling folk dances with a ceilidh band.

Copyright 2000 by Mike Salter First published December 2000.
Folly Publications, Folly Cottage, 151 West Malvern Rd, Malvern, Worcs WR14 4AY
Printed by Aspect Design, 89 Newtown Rd, Malvern, Worcs, WR14 2PD

Crowhurst Church

CONTENTS

Inside the front cover is a map of churches in the gazetteer.

INTRODUCTION

In Saxon times Surrey formed part of the kingdom of Wessex and until a cathedral was created at Guildford in 1927 Surrey was part of the diocese of Winchester. Several Saxon kings were crowned at Kingston-on-Thames but nothing of that period remains there. Saxon structural remains in Surrey churches dating from the late 10th century or early to mid 11th century can be seen in the chancels at Godalming and Thursley, the central tower at St Mary's at Guildford, the nave at Witley, the nave at Albury, a single loose capital at Betchworth, a window with re-used Roman bricks at Fetcham, and parts of a nave and chancel at Stoke D'Abernon. The first four of these have windows set in the middle of the thickness of the walls with the embrasures splayed both towards the interior and exterior. Surrey was heavily wooded in the medieval period and still contains a lot of woodland. It is likely that several churches of the Saxon period were entirely of wood and indeed a timber-framed church from as late as 1606 survived at Frimley until 1825. Other churches have been so extended and rebuilt over the years that no early parts now remain in them.

The parochial system began to take shape in the Saxon period but crystallised during the century and a half after the Norman Conquest of 1066. Between the early 13th century and when London began to encroach on the NE corner of Surrey in the early 19th century few entirely new churches were erected. The county contains about a hundred churches which are still essentially medieval, and another thirty which are of medieval origin but little or nothing of the medieval structure survives. Nearly fifty churches have some relic of the period 1070-1200, although in some cases it is no more than a font or a reset doorway or window. Farleigh is a comparatively unaltered example of a humble 12th century village church. It consisted of a nave about twice as long as it is wide inside and a narrower square chancel. The two parts were linked by a round chancel arch, since widened and there were two windows on each side of the nave and one on each side of the chancel, with another in the now-lost original east wall of the chancel. These round-arched windows were just small loops admitting minimal light. The nave has round-arched doorways facing west and south. A single bell sits in a timber-framed turret perched on the west end of the nave roof. Similarly little unaltered nave-and-chancel churches survive at Pyrford and Wisley. Ewhurst has a particularly monumental south doorway of the early 12th century, whilst Limpsfield has herringbone masonry, slabs in alternate directions laid at 45 degrees.

13th century doorway, Merstham

Norman doorway at Chipstead

Interior of Compton Church

Compton has the very rare feature of a two storey chancel, the lower level being vaulted and the upper level having an original 12th century timber balustrade, a unique survival. The chancel at Ripley was also intended to be vaulted. By the late 12th century St Mary's at Guildford was cruciform with an aisled nave, transepts, and a chancel with north and south chapels, all three having east apses, a feature more usual in the late 11th century and early 12th century rather than as late as the 1180s. Most apses were later replaced by straight east ends but here all three survived until the chancel apse was removed for road widening in the 19th century. Norman doorways often have zig-zag or chevron ornamentation, like those at Compton, Cobham and Pyrford. At Merton and Shere diamond shapes are broken around the edge of the order. However, Norman church doorways in Surrey are fairly modest compared with the rich displays found on doorways in other counties.

St Mary's at Guildford has a central tower of Saxon origin. Several other churches have Norman central towers, that at Albury being built over a Saxon chancel. Transepts are not common in Surrey churches so few of these churches were cruciform. Less than a quarter of the churches described in the gazetteer have a medieval tower at the west end of the nave and from the three centuries between 1300 and 1600 there are only about twenty towers, a remarkably low number. A few churches gained towers during 18th and 19th century rebuilding but there are many churches in Surrey that still have some sort of modest bellcote perched on the nave roof at or near the west end. Most of them are timber framed and have broach-spires covered with shingles. They can be of any date from the 13th century to the 17th and in any case most of them have been much renewed or altered over the years. Some bellcotes are supported on cross-braced timber posts inside the nave. At Thursley there is a massive arch-braced frame of 15th century date set halfway along the length of the nave, whilst Burstow has a timber framed west tower which is aisled to the north, west and south like some of the towers in Essex.

As the years rolled by simple nave and chancel churches were enlarged by adding aisles, but many churches remained of modest size until the end of the medieval period. About a dozen Surrey churches possessed at least one aisle by the year 1200, and arcades of round arches on circular piers with scalloped capitals remain at Chobham, Fetcham, St Mary's at Guildford, Great Bookham, Laleham, Little Bookham (now blocked up), Mickleham, Puttenham, and Walton on Thames, whilst the arcades at Compton have capitals with foliage and crockets on the piers. Of the end of the 12th century are arcades at Banstead, Carshalton and Reigate with crockets or stiff-leaf on the capitals. Entirely new aisles of the 14th, 15th and early 16th centuries are not common in Surrey churches, although there are several instances of narrow 12th and 13th century aisles being rebuilt wider later on, the original arcades sometimes partly or wholly surviving. Wanborough is a little altered 13th century single chamber, and others of that period at Oakwood and Warlingham remained like that until each was given an aisle in the 19th century. Modest 13th century chancels remain at Bramley and Byfleet, whilst Dunsfold is a complete late 13th century cruciform church with small transepts flanking the east end of the nave. Chipstead is a cruciform 13th century church on a more ambitious scale with a central tower and south aisle, whilst Merstham has a fine west tower and an aisled nave of that period. There are 13th century vaults over the chancels at St Mary at Guildford and Stoke D'Abernon, whilst chancels at Bletchingley, Chertsey and Merton have internal blind arcading.

Betchworth Church

Lingfield Church

Little 14th century work in Surrey parish churches calls for comment here. There are a few windows here and there, the odd aisle, porch, chapel or tower of no great distinction but no complete or even almost complete buildings except for the ruined chantry chapel of St Catherine near Guildford, and the tower, aisles and chancel at Cranleigh. The legacy of the period from 1400 up to the time of the Reformation of the 1530s and 40s in Surrey churches is almost as barren. However, there are over a dozen towers of this period, mostly of the type with diagonal buttresses at the western corners and a stair turret rising above the main parapet at one of the eastern corners, although that at Farnham has polygonal corner turrets. The collegiate church at Lingfield is mostly 15th century and has arcades with the then normal section of four shafts with four hollows between them. Otherwise there is the usual selection of bits and pieces, much of it rebuilding or enlargement of earlier work. There are stone porches at Merstham and Oxted and wooden porches at Bisley, Elstead and Egham, the latter now moved across the churchyard to serve as a lych gate.

English churches as a whole tend to have plenty of furnishings and monuments of the late 16th and 17th centuries but not much architecture, and this is true of Surrey, although Maldon and Morden both have 17th century brick naves and towers. There is more from the 18th century, but the only important church of that period is Holy Trinity at Guildford. The churches at Kew, Richmond and Sunbury have been much altered, Pirbright is attractive but not important, Long Ditton has gone, and Wonersh is rather in the nature of a curious patch-up repair job. The numerous new 19th century churches lie outside the main scope of this book.

Dunsfold Church   *Albury Old Church*

Doorways and masonry styles can help to date the different parts of old churches but usually the shape and style of the windows is the best evidence. However it should always be remembered that windows may be later insertions in an older wall or earlier openings moved from elsewhere. The few 12th century windows surviving in Surrey churches are small and unremarkable. After 1200 windows were given pointed heads and made longer, producing what is commonly called a lancet. Initially they were used singly except for in the east wall of chancels where stepped groups of three were the norm in the 13th century, although at Farleigh and East Clandon there are pairs, a pattern used in some 12th century chancels. Ockham has an east window of seven stepped lancets probably from Newark Priory and replacing an original triplet. By the mid 13th century pairs of lancets began to appear in other parts of churches and then eventually the spandrel between the heads was pierced with a circle. The next stage is seen at Dunsfold c1270 where the circles enclose trefoils. Of the end of the 13th century are the Geometrical style windows at Albury and Godalming, of five and four lights respectively with two tiers of circles of quatrefoils above. Dating from the same period are the two-light windows with Y-tracery at Byfleet. This motif used in a window with more lights, as in the east wall of the same church, produces intersecting tracery. Albury has a variant on Y-tracery where the two lights have heads of their own broken away from the side of the window.

The largest and finest type of Decorated style 14th century window is absent in Surrey. The best windows of this period are those with the Kent motif of a topmost quatrefoil at Charlwood and Horley, and those with curvilinear tracery forms at Old Woking, Shere, Worpleston and Witley. The chancel of the 1340s at Great Bookham has reticulated tracery in the east window and cusped Y-tracery in the side windows. Cranleigh has square-headed windows with pairs of ogival-headed lights, whilst Thorpe has single-light windows with trefoils and quatrefoils in the heads. Effingham has two-light windows under segmental heads dating from c1390 and there are similar examples at Beddington. Common 15th century types have three lights splitting into six small lights in the head or three lights under a segmental head. Eventually the lights are given arched heads with cusping and then in the early 16th century the cusping went out of fashion. By 1600 round arches were back in fashion.

Great Bookham Church

Beddington Church

Addington Church

West Horsley Church

Bisley Church

Horne Church

Newdigate Church

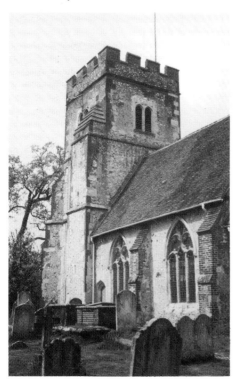

Ockham Church

Beddington Church

Burstow Church

Worpleston Church

By the time of the Reformation of the 1530s the interiors of churches that had been bare and poorly lighted in the 12th and early 13th centuries had been transformed. Large new windows admitted more light, despite often being filled with stained glass. About twenty churches in Surrey have old stained glass although some of it has come from elsewhere, and there is little to show for the fact that Chiddingfold was an important centre for glass-making in the medieval period. A fair amount of old glass was brought to Surrey from Continental churches during the 19th century, along with a number of other furnishings, Gatton being particularly rich in foreign furnishings. Internal walls were usually whitewashed and then painted with biblical scenes or lives of saints. There is a very fine scene of c1200 showing Purgatory and Hell taking up most of the nave west wall at Chaldon, and there are other wall paintings of note at Pyrford, Stoke D'Abernon and Witley, plus faded fragments in a few other churches. In the early medieval period the congregation would stand during the services but later on benches were provided, those at Dunsfold being probably as early as the 1270s, whilst Littleton has late medieval pews. The larger churches had choir stalls with miserichords or hinged seats with lips to support the behinds of choristers when standing. Sets of them survive at Beddington and Lingfield. The growth of choirs is one reason why chancels were often enlarged later on in the medieval period. Chancels often had built into the south wall (sometimes in conjunction with a window embrasure) two or three seats called sedilia for the use of the clergy. Just to the east of the sedilia would be the piscina or basin used for rinsing and draining the mass vessels.

Old doors survive occasionally but more common is the reuse of medieval ironwork on a more recent door. Patterned medieval floor tiles also sometimes remain, especially on the raised step for the altar. Several churches have 17th or 18th century wooden rails either closing off the altar step entirely or returning along the sides to surround three sides of the altar. Medieval pulpits are rare (the one at Gatton is from abroad) and indeed lengthy sermons only became the norm in the 16th century when English replaced Latin as the liturgical language and at last commoners could understand all that was being said during the services. Elizabethan pulpits are equally rare in Surrey but there are a dozen 17th century examples and a few from the 18th century, the rest being more recent.

Pulpit at Chaldon

In the later medieval period it was normal for chancels and chapels to be divided off by screens in the form of traceried timber partitions. The screen dividing off the chancel from the nave was often surmounted by a loft reached by a staircase in a sidewall, although few examples of such stairs remain in Surrey and no lofts now remain. Towards the nave the loft would have a parapet upon which was mounted a rood or crucifix, hence the terms rood-loft and rood-screen. The loft was used by musicians (important in an age when few churches could afford an organ), and by the performers of religious plays which were an important means of conveying biblical ideas to a congregation containing many who could neither read or write nor understand spoken Latin. Old screens remain at Charlwood, Chipstead, Ewell, Gatton, Littleton, Nutfield, Reigate, and Wanborough, although some of them have been heavily restored. Of these the best are at Charlwood and Gatton, the latter an import from another church somewhere else in SE England.

Wooden grave marker at Mickleham

Font at Lingfield

Font at Limpsfield

Alfold and Thursley and a few other places have plain Norman fonts. At Thames Ditton there is a Norman font like a block capital. By far the most important font in Surrey is one of lead at Walton-on-the-Hill with saints in relief under arcading on the side of the bowl. There are only a few 13th century fonts and although there are rather more from the 15th and 17th centuries none need to be singled out here.

Farnham Church

Porch at Merton

Surrey has very few stone effigies earlier than the 17th century. There are figures of medieval priests at Walton-on-the-Hill and West Horsley, and there is a knight at Horley, but these are overshadowed by two knights of the 14th and 15th century respectively at Lingfield. As with all the other counties close both to London and the Continent there is a large collection of engraved brass memorials in Surrey. Stoke D'Abernon has the earliest brass in England, a knight who died in 1277 shown with the unique feature of a lance, and there is a second knight of the early 14th century. There are more than forty brasses dating from the 15th century, and there are nearly sixty from the 16th century. Many of them are quite small and there are a number of half-figures, especially of priests. A large number are family groups, but with the figures of the husband, wife and groups of children of each sex cut out separately and set into indents. Occasionally indents survive without the brasses. Some brasses are set on the tops of tomb chests or in tomb recesses but the majority originally lay on the floor, although during the 19th and 20th centuries many of these were transferred to the walls to avoid them being worn out or covered by furniture. In the 16th century figures are often shown kneeling towards each other, sometimes with a prayer desk between them and the boys behind the husband and the girls behind the wife. Several stone monuments of this period also have this layout of figures. Good late 16th century tombs appear at Bletchingley and Cheam.

Brass at Croydon   *Brass at Crowhurst*   *Brass at Lingfield*

Tablet at Chaldon

Effigy at Great Bookham

Brass at East Horsley

Brass at Thames Ditton

About sixty 17th century monuments are mentioned in the gazetteers and over seventy from the 18th century. In addition there are some minor monuments and a few where the inscriptions are now difficult to read. About a dozen of the 17th century monuments are brasses, another dozen are recumbent effigies and a similar number have kneeling figures, but the emphasis on effigies gradually decreased during the 17th century. Later monuments most commonly take the form of a tablet mounted on a wall and having a long inscription with or without an architectural surround adorned with urns, fruit, goddesses, cherubs, symbols of death or images relating to a profession or claim to fame. Good early 17th century monuments appear at Addington, Croydon, East Horsley, Egham, Holy Trinity at Guildford and Stoke D'Abernon. The Baroque style first appears in monuments by Bushnell at Peter Harrow, c1680. There are good monuments of the 1690s at Epsom, and Mortlake, and of the early 18th century at Bletchingley, Capel, Carshalton, Ewell, Great Bookham, Leatherhead, and West Horsley. Monuments of the 1730s at Ockham and Reigate show the deceased in Roman dress. Although the surviving examples lie beyond the post 1800 cut-off point for this book, the Surrey fashion for marking graves in churchyards with a long plank between two posts is worth noting here.

GAZETTEER OF OLD CHURCHES IN SURREY

ABINGER   *St James*   TQ 115460

A shingled bell-turret has replaced a weather-boarded turret destroyed by bombing during World War II. The nave has Norman windows and the chancel is 13th century but several restorations, the most recent in 1964 after a fire, have removed most of the ancient features and the north chapel is entirely modern. In the south porch is a 15th century relief of the Crucifixion from a Nottingham workshop.

ADDINGTON   *St Mary*   TQ 371641

The Norman chancel has original single windows on the north and south (the latter now blocked), and three renewed ones in the east wall. The tower was rebuilt in 1773 and the wide north aisle and north vestry are of the restoration by St Aubyn in 1876, but the masonry and three bay arcade of the south aisle with double-chamfered arches on octagonal piers are 13th century. There are brasses to John Leigh, d1509, and his wife Isabel, d1544, and Thomas Hatteclyff, d1540. There are semi-reclining and kneeling figures of Sir Illiphe Leigh, d1612, and his wife, his parents, and grandparents. Mrs Lovell and Mrs Leigh, both d1691, have a joint monument. There are other memorials to Grizel Trecothick, d1769, and Barlow Trecothick, Lord Mayor of London, d1775.

Albury Old Church

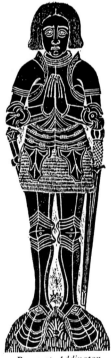

Brass at Addington

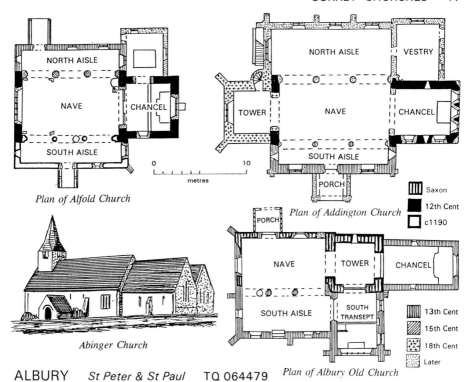

Plan of Alfold Church

Plan of Addington Church

Abinger Church

Plan of Albury Old Church

	Saxon
	12th Cent
	c1190
	13th Cent
	15th Cent
	18th Cent
	Later

ALBURY   St Peter & St Paul   TQ 064479

Much of a Saxon nave and chancel still survive in the disused old church by Albury Park, although the chancel was converted into a tower by thickening the walls externally in the 12th century, the period of the east and west tower arches. The tower north window is original Saxon work with a Norman outer opening. The recently re-roofed 13th century chancel has an east window of c1500. At the end of the 13th century a narrow aisle of c1200 was replaced by the present wide aisle and a south transept added. There are two-light windows with Y-tracery, a large five-light window, and a three bay arcade, plus traces of a wall-painting of St Christopher. The cupola and parapet on the tower were added in 1820 to replace a collapsed later medieval spire. The north porch with a delicately carved barge board is of c1500, but the doorway is 13th century. In the aisle is a tomb slab of William Weston, c1330, and a brass to John Weston, d1440. There are several modest 17th century tablets and also a larger monument to Sir Robert Godschall, d1742.

ALFOLD   St Nicholas   TQ 037340

The church has a big roof covering both nave and aisles in one, and several late 13th century windows in the form of twinned or cusped lancets. The late 12th century south arcade has pointed arches without chamfers on circular piers. The north arcade and the chancel arch are early 14th century. Several windows and the wooden south porch are also 14th century. The tub font with Maltese crosses set in arches with a thick cable-moulding round the base is late 11th century. The shingled bell-chamber is carried on a 15th century wooden frame with big corner posts and curved braces supporting horizontal beams. There is a Jacobean pulpit with a tester.

ASH   *St Peter*   SU 898508

The north aisle of 1865 (now used as the nave) contains a reset small Norman window and there is a fine south doorway of c1200, round-headed with stiff-leaf capitals. The chancel contains one 13th century lancet on the south side. The south porch of timber and brick is 16th century whilst the tower is 15th century, but carries a 19th century shingle spire. Under the tower are Royal Arms of George III. The 17th century wooden font has an octagonal bowl on eight octagonal columns and a round central post. In the chancel is a tablet of 1759 to John Harris.

ASHFORD   *St Matthew*   TQ 073715

The existing church with a tower beyond the south aisle is of 1858-65 by Butterfield. It contains a brass to William Goode, d1522 and his wife from the old church whose Norman chancel (marked on the ground by a floor slab) lay east of the new church.

ASHTEAD   *St Giles*   193580

Most of the church was rebuilt in 1862 when a north transept was added, but the diagonally buttressed tower with a square stair-turret is 16th century. The vestry was added in 1891. The east window contains 16th century Belgian stained glass showing the Crucifixion and there is an octagonal 15th century font with quatrefoils. There are several late 17th and early 18th century tablets, the best being those of Henry Newdigate, d1629 (but the monument made in 1693), Thomas Howard, d1701, Sarah Bond, d1712, and Diana Fielding, d1733.

BANSTEAD   *All Saints*   TQ 255596

The two bay north arcade of c1200 has unchamfered arches on an octagonal pier and responds with crocketted capitals. Of the early 13th century are the west tower with a later shingled spire and angle buttresses, the chancel arch and chancel inclined to the south, plus the two bay arcades towards the chapels. In these parts all the arches have chamfers, as does the small arch east of the older arcade. The chapel arcade piers have crocket capitals, the pier on the north being octagonal with sunk sides. The octagonal font with tracery panels is 15th century. A tablet has a figure of the baby Paul Tracey, d1618 in a chrisom robe. There are monuments to Elizabeth Till, d1748, Daniel Lambert, former mayor of London, d1750, Nicholas Lambert, d1755, and Daniel Lambert, d1768, plus several others under the tower.

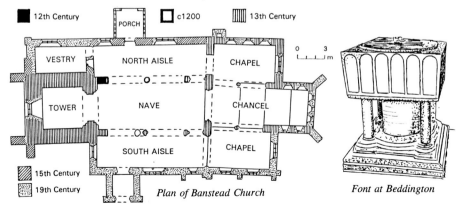

Plan of Banstead Church   *Font at Beddington*

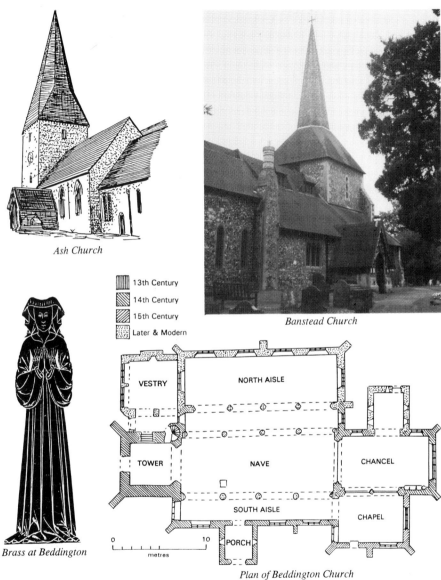

Ash Church

Banstead Church

13th Century
14th Century
15th Century
Later & Modern

VESTRY

NORTH AISLE

TOWER

NAVE

CHANCEL

SOUTH AISLE

CHAPEL

PORCH

0   10
metres

Brass at Beddington

Plan of Beddington Church

BARNES   *St Mary*   TQ 223766

The church was gutted by fire in 1978 and was rebuilt in 1983-4, whilst the tower, originally 17th century but restored in 1838 and 1853, was rebuilt in 1990. The rebuilt church has been re-orientated and now has the altar on the north side, beyond which is a complex of modern rooms. Three renewed east lancets with later bricks between them survive from the 13th century chancel. The oldest monuments are a brass to Edith and Elizabeth, daughters of John Wylde "which died virgyns" in 1508 and a mourning woman and child to Sir Richard Hoare of Barn Elms, d1787.

Beddington Church

BEDDINGTON   *St Mary*   TQ 295653

The arcades with renewed octagonal piers with long diagonals may be 13th century and older masonry probably survives in the nave. The aisles are early 14th century. One window of that period remains on the north side and another is reset in the west wall of the early 15th century Carew chapel. The chapel is of two bays with a pier of the four-shafts-and-four-hollows type. The tower and porch, and perhaps also the chancel, were built with funds left by Sir Nicholas Carew, d1390. An outer north aisle was added during a restoration of 1850 by Clarke, and the west vestries, chancel arch, and the roofs of the nave and chancel are of 1869 by the same architect. The dormer windows, however, were inserted c1913. The square font on five supports with shallow blank arcading on the bowl is 13th century. The pulpit of 1611 has linenfold panels and posts with arabesques. Nine of the chancel stalls have medieval miserichords carved with shields, foliage and two heads. Three brasses lying hidden under these stalls depict Philip Carew, d1414, with half effigies of her brothers and sisters, Thomas Carew, d1430 and his sister Isabel, and Roger Elmebrygge, Sheriff of Surrey and Sussex, d1437, and there is a cross to Margaret Oliver, d1425. There are other brasses to Nicholas Carew, d1432, and his wife Isabel, Katheryn Berecroft and her sister Elizabeth, both d1507, and Sir Richard Carew, d1520, and his wife Malin, the last of these on a fine tomb in the chapel. There is also a recumbent effigy of Sir Francis Carew, d1611.

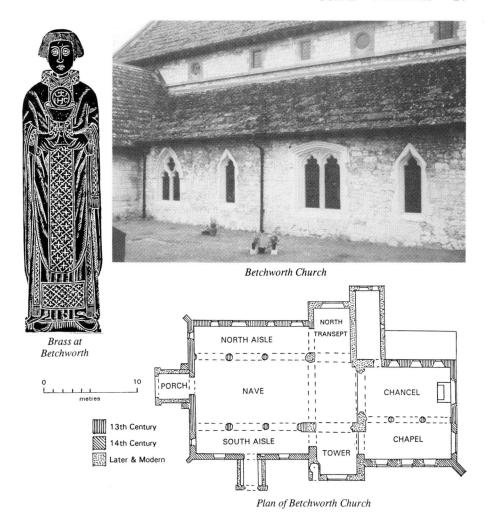

Betchworth Church

*Brass at
Betchworth*

0 ——————— 10
metres

13th Century
14th Century
Later & Modern

NORTH AISLE
NORTH
TRANSEPT
PORCH
NAVE
CHANCEL
SOUTH AISLE
CHAPEL
TOWER

Plan of Betchworth Church

BETCHWORTH   *St Michael*   T.Q 211498

In 1851 E.C.Hakewill removed a Norman crossing tower and erected a new tower over the south transept. This tower has a late 11th century arch towards the aisle and a late 12th century arch facing east. Reset on the tower south window is a capital of c1000 with eight circular roll-mouldings, one above another. The arcade between the chancel and south chapel is early 13th century with two orders of arches, only one chamfered, on round piers with octagonal abaci. The nave arcades are also 13th century, but the north arcade thicker piers is earlier, the south arcade having one of the two piers octagonal, and the responds are semi-octagonal. The irregular circular openings of the clerestory could be of almost any date from the 13th century onwards. Both aisles and the south chapel contain several 14th century windows. There is an ancient dug-out chest with seven iron staples. The best monuments are Victorian but there is a brass of vicar Thomas Wardysworth, d1533.

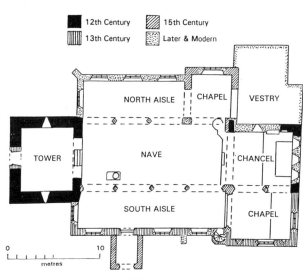

■ 12th Century	▨ 15th Century
▥ 13th Century	▦ Later & Modern

Bletchingley Church

Plan of Bletchingley Church

BISLEY   *St John Baptist*   SU 958596

A shingled belfry stands on 14th century framing inside the 13th century nave, and there is a fine timber late 14th century west porch. An early 19th century chancel has replaced a former timber-framed chancel, and a north aisle was added in 1873. The octagonal font has foiled panels containing crosses in roundels.

BLETCHINGLEY   *St Mary*   TQ 327508

The unusually large west tower is Norman with original windows on three sides and shafts on the tower arch responds. The 17th century top stage was rebuilt in 1910. The chancel has 13th century north lancets set in Norman walling. The east lancets of 1870 replace a 15th century window. The south aisle and wider south chapel have 13th century walling, with one blocked lancet in the chapel and a doorway in the aisle. The two-storied porch is 15th century, as are the chapel windows, the north transept, the south arcade and the octagonal font with quatrefoils on the bowl and trefoiled-headed niches on the stem. The north aisle and south windows are of 1856 by Rhode Hawkins. The pulpit was given in 1630. There are brasses of various sets of children, a 15th century female, and 15th century figures reused to represent Thomas Warde, d1541, and his wife Joan. There is only an inscription on the plate on the tomb chest of Anne of Cleves' steward Sir Thomas Cawarden, d1559. There is also a fine monument in the south chapel to Sir Robert Clayton, d1707, Lord Mayor of London, and a cherub with an urn in a niche to Lady Clayton, d1772.

BRAMLEY   *Holy Trinity*   TQ 009449

The chancel of c1220 remains complete with triple east lancets. The rest was rebuilt in 1850 and 1876, although the arch of the west doorway contains Norman work. In the south aisle is a monument to Henry Ludlow, d1730.

Burstow Church

BUCKLAND   *St Mary*   TQ 222508

The church and many of the furnishings essentially date from the 1860 rebuilding by
Woodyer but the timber-framed bellcote on four posts is medieval, and one window
in the nave has 14th century stained glass rivalling Hardman's chancel windows.

BURSTOW   *St Bartholomew*   TQ 313414

The timber framed west tower has narrow aisles on all four sides and diagonal
bracing. The lean-to aisle roof conceals buttressing for the upper levels. The top part
is battered and has a broach-spire and four corner pinnacles with shingles. The west
doorway suggests a 16th century date, but the upper parts may be 18th century
remodelling. The nave and chancel each have one Norman north window, the latter
now looking into a Victorian vestry. The chancel was rebuilt longer in the 15th
century, when a south aisle with a three bay arcade was added. Both chancel and
aisle have a four-light south window. Also of this period are the chancel arch flanked
by niches, the piscina and the octagonal font with quatrefoils on the bowl sides and
leaves underneath. The large iron-bound chest is probably of c1600.

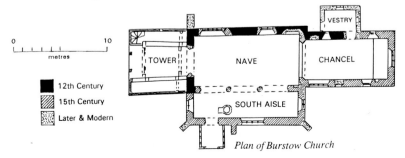

Plan of Burstow Church

Byfleet Church

Chancel at Byfleet

BYFLEET   *St Mary*   TQ 064604

The addition of a south aisle of 1841 and a south transept by Woodyer in 1864 has rather spoiled a simple nave and chancel church of the 1290s with a chancel arch with an inner order carried on corbels, two light windows with Y-tracery and a three-light west window with intersecting tracery. There are very slight traces of wall paintings over the north doorway. The pulpit is Jacobean but has been altered. There is a brass of c1480 to Thomas Teylar, Rector of Byfleet. One chancel window contains a medieval stained glass figure of a saint.

CAPEL   *St John the Baptist*

TQ 176408

The chancel has 13th century south lancets but the church was mostly rebuilt in 1865 by Woodyer, who added a north aisle. Late medieval are the SE buttress of the nave, the west porch and the wooden frame which carries on two posts the shingled bell-turret. Lying outside is the base of an old font with five supporting columns. There are kneeling effigies of John Cowper, d1590 and his wife, and there is a Baroque style tablet to Robert Cowper, d1720.

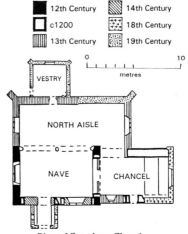

Plan of Caterham Church

Chaldon Church

Carshalton Church

CARSHALTON   *All Saints*   TQ 280646

Much of the large church is the work of Sir Arthur Blomfield and his nephew between 1893 and 1914. On the south side, hidden from the High Street, are the older parts. The chancel of c1200 (now the Lady Chapel) has its lancets now obliterated and the 15th century east window blocked, although the two-light side windows on the south remain in use. This part has a rounded-trefoil headed piscina, a king-post roof and an early 18th century altar rail. West of it is a Norman central tower. The nave beyond it is now swallowed into the Victorian south aisle, alongside which is the late 12th century original south aisle with a three bay arcade of double-chamfered pointed arches on octagonal piers with crocket capitals. The aisle has a blocked late medieval south doorway and was heightened and the south wall partly rebuilt in 1723. The Georgian pulpit was modified in 1946. The many monuments include a tomb chest with kneeling brasses (originally enamelled) of Nicholas Gaynesford, d1497, and his wife Margaret, brasses of Thomas Elyngbrigge, d1497, and his wife Elizabeth, a brass of the priest Walter Gaynesford, d1493, a brass to Joan Burton, d1524, a tablet to Dorothy Burrish, d1685, a tablet to Henry Herringman, d1703, with putti keeping a curtain open, a wall-monument to Sir John Fellowes, a reclining effigy of Sir William Scawen, d1722, a tablet of 1753 to John Braddyll, and an urn in a plain niche to Sir George Amyand, d1766.

CATERHAM   *St Lawrence*   TQ 335564

On the south side are traces of the beginning of a former Norman apse and part of a window of that period. Chapels were added c1200, then a south aisle with a now-blocked arcade of two bays of plain arches with an oblong pier between them, and then a north aisle of double-chamfered arches on circular piers. The chancel arch is probably mid 13th century. The present east end of clunch and brick is of c1790. The nave has a king-post roof, the chancel a wagon roof and the aisle a queen-post roof. The church was disused after a new church of St Mary was built opposite to it in 1866-88 by W. Basset Smith, but it was refitted for occasional use in 1927. From it has come a 13th century font in the church of St John of 1881 in Caterham Valley.

Wall painting at Chaldon Church

CHALDON   *St Peter & St Paul*   TQ 309557

This church is famous for the wall painting of c1200 on the nave west wall with ochre-coloured figures set against a dark red background. It shows Purgatory above Hell and has naked bodies scrambling up a ladder connecting them. Hell has a cauldron attended by devils. Other devils hold a saw on which people unsuccessfully try to carry on their trades, for the potter has no wheel, and the blacksmiths no anvil. The Seven Deadly Sins are inserted wherever there is room for them. Sloth has souls trying to walk on a beast instead of the ground, Gluttony has a pilgrim throwing away his coat and bourdon and grasping a bottle, Pride a beast grasping a woman's arm, Anger two struggling figures, Luxury an embracing couple with a devil about to interfere, Avarice a figure weighed down with money-bags, and Envy a devil preventing one figure attracting another. There is also a Tree of Good and Evil with the Serpent, above which is Christ in Limbo. Another scene shows Archangel Michael weighing souls.

The church is quite small and has late 11th century masonry in the nave and chancel, with one original window above the wall-painting. A north chapel was removed in the 14th century and the 13th century north aisle then rebuilt except for the arcade of double-chamfered arches. The south chapel has 14th century features but the masonry seems to be late 12th century, the period of the narrow south aisle with a two bay arcade with slightly chamfered arches on a circular pier. The south porch is 16th century. In 1843 a small tower with a shingle broach-spire was built over the south aisle west end. In the chancel are a late medieval Easter sepulchre with quatrefoils and shields and a tablet dated 1562. The pulpit is dated 1657.

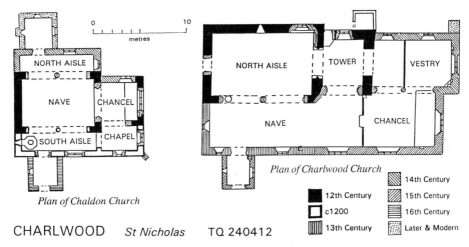

0   10
metres

NORTH AISLE

NAVE   CHANCEL

SOUTH AISLE   CHAPEL

Plan of Chaldon Church

NORTH AISLE   TOWER   VESTRY

NAVE   CHANCEL

Plan of Charlwood Church

	12th Century
	c1200
	13th Century

	14th Century
	15th Century
	16th Century
	Later & Modern

CHARLWOOD   *St Nicholas*   TQ 240412

The original nave has one Norman north window and the central tower is also Norman. The original early 14th century chancel has two 15th century windows and is now subdivided to provide vestries. The nave has one good 14th century north window. The present nave and chancel were originally a late 13th century south aisle with one original window which was extended to form a south chapel in the late 15th century. A screen dividing the two parts has initials of Richard Sander, d1480. Of that period are the south arch of the tower, the arcade of four-centred arches between the chancel and chapel, and probably the king-post roofs. On the south wall are slight traces of wall paintings of the Three Quick and the Three Dead. The 15th century south porch has a quatrefoil west window. The octagonal font is probably 17th century. There is a brass to Nicholas Sander, d1553, and his wife Alice.

Charlwood Church

CHEAM   *St Dunstan*   TQ 243640

The Lumley Chapel in the churchyard was part of the old church, replaced by that built in 1862-4 by Powell. It has a renewed 16th century east window and a blocked 13th century arch to the former chancel. The roof is of 1592. The chapel contains brasses of two civilians of c1390, tiny late 15th century figures of John Yerde, d1449, and his wife Anne, half figures of John Compton, d1450 and his wife Joan, d1458, and William Wodeward, d1459, figures of Thomas Fromonde, d1542, and his wife Elizabeth, which are palimpsests with on the reverse kneeling figures, a St John the Evangelist of c1420 and a scroll and heart of c1500. Other monuments include alabaster panels with a kneeling figure of Lady Jane Lumley, d1577, a recumbent effigy of Lady Elizabeth Lumley, d1603, made before her death, and a an inscription with columns to John, Lord Lumley, d1609.

CHELSHAM   *St Leonard*   TQ 388591

The chancel and all the external features were renewed in 1870-1 by Spencer, when the two north vestries were added. Herringbone masonry in the chancel suggests Early Norman work there, but the shaft in the SE corner and renewed lancets are part of a 13th century remodelling. Until 1870 most of the nave and tower were 13th century, and there is a square font with corner shafts of that period. The chancel screen is work of c1530 re-used from a former parclose screen in the nave.

CHERTSEY   *St Peter*   TQ 043671

The nave and aisles were rebuilt in 1806-8 to a design by Richard Elsam. The tower and the chancel have 15th century features internally, but possibly older masonry. The chancel has two-bay wall arcades inside with shallow cinque-foiled niches above them, and contains a few poor-quality tiles from the vanished abbey of Chertsey. There are monuments to Pratt Mawbey, d1770, and Sir Joseph Mawbey, d1798, amongst a group of several late 18th century tablets of no importance.

Chelsham Church

CHESSINGTON   *St Mary*   TQ 185635

The nave and chancel have narrow lancets of c1200 with round rere-arches inside. The sedilia are just two blank arches. The east window is probably 17th century. The broach-spire on the bell-turret was restored in 1854 and the south aisle was built in 1870 by Jackson. It has the original south doorway reset in it and a wooden arcade of three bays. There is a 15th century panel showing the Annunciation.

CHIDDINGFOLD   *St Mary*   SU 961354

Lumley Chapel, Cheam

Of the 13th century are the chancel with a group of three lancets on the south side and a two bay arcade towards the north chapel, and possibly the west tower, although the Victoria County History calls it 17th century, and the top is of 1869-70. The arcades contain 13th century material in the arches and columns but seem to have been remodelled in the 15th century. The external details are mostly of the restoration of 1869 by Henry Woodyer. The nave contains a chandelier dated 1786. In the south aisle are several late 18th century tablets.

Chiddingfold Church

Chertsey Church

Chilworth Church

CHILWORTH   *St Martha*   TQ 027484

The church lies entirely alone on a hilltop only reached by paths. It was rebuilt from a state of ruin by Henry Woodyer in 1848-50, and the 12th century tub font was then brought in from Hambledon. The nave is mostly Woodyer's except for the mostly renewed arch of a former west tower. The church has a crossing with four pointed arches and transepts of the 1190s but had no central tower until the restoration. The chancel is 13th century with renewed lancets to north and south.

CHIPSTEAD   *St Margaret*   TQ 284565

The church has a central tower with transepts, a chancel with five lancets on the north side and four plus a doorway and piscina on the south, and a south aisle with a four bay arcade of double-chamfered arches on circular piers. All this is 13th century except that the south transept was mostly rebuilt in 1855 and Norman work survives in the nave west wall. The lancets in the chancel and north transept have triangular rere-arches. The transept west doorway has a similar head. It now opens into a north aisle of 1883 in which is reset a Norman doorway. Over the transept west doorway and over its three north lancets are single oculus windows. The tower is dated 1631. The chancel has old stone benches on each side. The octagonal font with tracery patterns is 14th century, although the base is of 1827. The screen under the east arch of the tower is 15th century, and a little of the glass in the east window is of that period. There is a Jacobean font. On the chancel floor is a brass to Lucy Roper, d1614 and there is a monument to the Reverend James Tattershall, d1784.

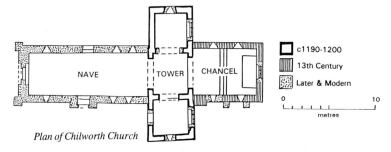

■ c1190-1200

▥ 13th Century

▨ Later & Modern

0 ————————— 10
metres

NAVE   TOWER   CHANCEL

Plan of Chilworth Church

Chipstead Church

CHOBHAM   *St Laurence*   SU 974618

The four bay south arcade with slightly chamfered pointed arches on circular piers is late 12th century. The western pier is square and a SW tower may have been intended. Over the arcade are older Norman windows. In the 15th century the diagonally buttressed west tower was added and the south aisle outer wall rebuilt with a rough chequerwork pattern. The west porch is also late medieval. A transeptal fifth bay beyond the arcade and the chancel were rebuilt in 1899, whilst the north aisle is of 1866. The nave and south aisle have a continuous roof. The wooden octagonal font bowl could be late medieval or post-Reformation. There is a 13th century chest with triple locks. The oldest monument is of Sir William Abdy, d1803.

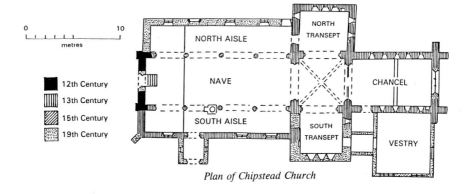

Plan of Chipstead Church

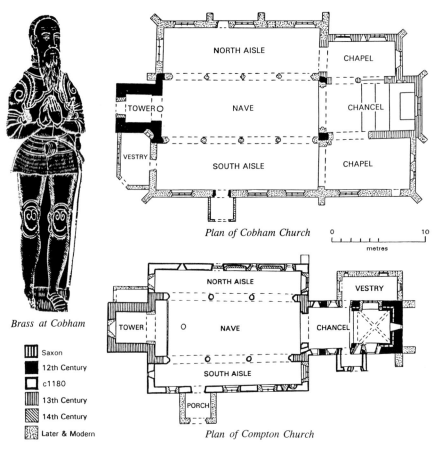

Brass at Cobham

Plan of Cobham Church

0   10
metres

▦ Saxon
■ 12th Century
☐ c1180
▥ 13th Century
▨ 14th Century
▩ Later & Modern

Plan of Compton Church

Compton Church

Coulsdon Church

Interior of Compton Church

COBHAM   *St Andrew*   TQ 108598

The west tower is Norman and has a tower arch on simple imposts with a scalloped frieze, but the quoins, the two-light bell-openings and the 15th century west doorway have all been renewed. The chancel and north chapel are 13th century with an original two bay arcade between them. The wide aisles and the spacious organ chamber on the south side are Victorian although the south windows are 15th century work reset and the south doorway is Norman, with one order of shafts with scalloped capitals, chevrons on the arch and billets on the hood-mould. The mid 16th century brass of a man in armour is a palimpsest with a priest on the reverse.

COMPTON   *St Nicholas*   SU 955470

The west tower and the chancel are 11th century work. The tower carries a shingled broach-spire of uncertain date. In the 1160s the chancel walls were thickened internally to carry a quadripartite vault, above which is an upper chapel with a an original wooden guard rail facing west with thin columns with crocket capitals. Both guard rail and two-storied sanctuary are very rare survivals. The aisles added in the 1180s have slightly pointed unchamfered arches. With them goes the chancel arch with nook-shafts and one order of chevrons. The west bay of the chancel has late 13th century lancets. The font of c1100 has a square bowl above a large circular stem and ring. The tower screen, altar rails and pulpit with tester are all Jacobean. The lower sanctuary east window has 13th century stained glass. The monument to Edward Fulham, d1694, and family in the porch was erected in 1778. On the nave floor is a brass to Thomas Gennyn (Jennings) and his wife Margaret, both d1508.

COULSDON   *St John Evangelist*   TQ 313582

Most of the south wall of the south aisle has been removed to give access into a large new church of 1958 extending to the south which rather dwarfs the old building. In the 13th century a late 11th century nave was given a new chancel with arcading and sedilia and piscina, plus north and south aisles of different widths. The west lancets of the aisles remain, although renewed. The north aisle was otherwise rebuilt wider in the 19th century. Of the 15th century are the two bay arcades and the angle-buttresses west tower. A spike has been added to the truncated pyramidal roof of the tower. There is a tablet to Grace Rowed, d1631.

CRANLEIGH   *St Nicholas*   TQ 060392

The church comprises a nave flanked by transepts, west of which are aisles with two wide bays, a large west tower with a big NW stair turret, and a chancel with triple sedilia and diagonal east buttresses. Much of it dates from c1330, with reticulated tracery in the south aisle west window, but the arcades appear to re-use the piers and responds of a late 12th century church with arcades of lower and narrower arches, and there is evidence of a former crossing. The transepts seem to be 13th century but were both lengthened in the restoration of 1864-6 when the south porch and north vestry and organ chamber were added. The south transept contains a 14th century screen. The late 16th century lectern with a twisted column on a strapwork base is of foreign workmanship. There are fragments of several brasses in the chancel, including a half-effigy of a priest of c1510 in the floor.

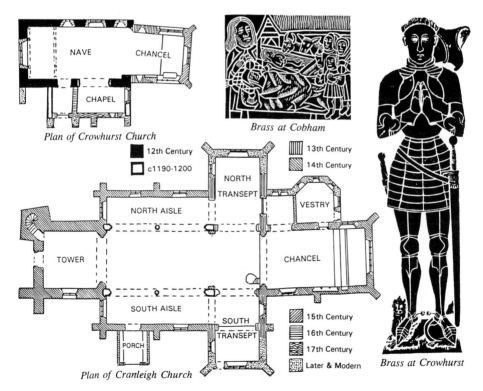

Plan of Crowhurst Church

Brass at Cobham

12th Century
c1190-1200
13th Century
14th Century
15th Century
16th Century
17th Century
Later & Modern

Plan of Cranleigh Church

Brass at Crowhurst

Brass at Cranleigh

Croydon Church

CROWHURST   *St George*   TQ 391475

This small chapel has a bell-turret carried on timber framing (restored 1947 after a fire) within the Norman nave. The chancel has a 13th century lancet on each side but the east end was rebuilt in the 15th century, the east window having fragments of glass of that date. The south aisle has a single slightly-chamfered and pointed arch of c1190. The repairs recorded in 1652 comprised the rebuilding of the aisle south wall and adjacent porch entrance. The nave has two later medieval windows. The 13th century font has an octagonal bowl broached from a larger square base. In the chancel are tomb chests with brasses of John Gaynesford, d1450, John Gaynesford, d1460, with a canopy, tablets to Thomasina Maryott, d1675, and Justinian Angell, d1680, and a cast-iron slab showing Anne Forster, d1591, in her burial shroud.

CROYDON   *St John the Baptist*   TQ 319654

This, the largest parish church in the county, thanks to the munificence of the archbishops of Canterbury, was destroyed by fire in 1867 and rebuilt in 1870 by Sir Giles Gilbert Scott, largely in imitation of the original. The nave originally had five bays but now has six and there is a two storey south porch. A late 15th century tomb recess survives in the north aisle and two large 14th century corbels, one of which has a head, remain at the west end of the south aisle. There is a fine late medieval brass lectern with an eagle top and three small lions at the base

DORKING   *St Martin*   TQ 116495

Except for a south chapel of 1912 this is a fine church of 1868-77 by Woodyer with a clerestory and a lofty tower and spire. From the old church there remain several old tablets set too high up in the tower for them to be seen properly and a font said to have come from Holland which contains a 17th century panel of St Martin and the beggar and late medieval figures of apostles and busts of angels.

DUNSFOLD   *St Mary & All Saints*   SU 998363

This is a complete cruciform church of the 1270s with angle buttresses, doorways with nook-shafts and two-light windows each with a circle containing a pointed trefoil. There are no aisles but the west respond of the south transept arch is a complete pier as if a south aisle was intended. On the north side of the chancel arch the nave has a squint into the chancel. Later only are the three-light west window with cusped intersecting tracery, the shingled bell-turret on a four post cage of the 15th century, resulting in the westernmost window on each side being blocked, and the 20th century north vestry. There are original sedilia and piscina and also a set of contemporary pews with the ends having a down-pointing cusp between two knobs. There are Royal Arms of George IV dated 1828.

EAST CLANDON   *St Thomas*   TQ 060518

The nave walling is probably Norman but the windows are 15th century. The 13th century chancel has two (not the usual three) east lancets. The north doorway has a shouldered lintel and must be slightly later. The arch between the nave and the aisle rebuilt in 1900 is also 13th century. The upper parts of the timber framed bell-turret were rebuilt in 1900. The font is 18th century and there are 17th century altar rails.

EAST HORSLEY   *St Martin*   TQ 095528

The tower is partly Norman with 13th century alterations and a 18th century top stage, now the only part still roughcasted. The rest of the church was 13th century but little apart from the chancel arch and the two westernmost bays of the 15th century arcade survived the restoration of 1869 by Henry Woodyer. There is a brass with a half-figure of the civilian Robert de Brantyngham, c1390. There are also brasses of John Bowthe, Bishop of Exeter, d1478, kneeling carrying a crozier, and John Snelling, d1498, with his wife Alice and family, and children from a brass to Thomas Snelling, d1504. There are also cartouches to Henry Hudeyard, d1674 and James ffox, d1753, plus recumbent effigies of Elizabeth I's Groom Porter Thomas Cornwallis, d1626, and his wife with kneeling figures of their children.

Dunsfold Church

East Horsley Church

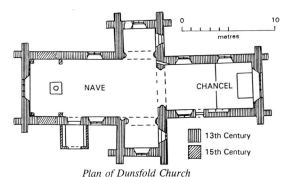

Plan of Dunsfold Church

Window at Effingham

EAST MOLESEY *St Mary* TQ 147679

The church was entirely rebuilt in 1864-7 by Talbot Bury and a south aisle was added in 1883 by Charles Barry. Inside are tablets and brasses from the old church.

EFFINGHAM *St Laurence* TQ 118537

The south transept of c1250 has a king-post roof. The east window is early 14th century but some of the side windows of the chancel with head-stops on the hoodmoulds are probably part of the work ordered in 1388 by William of Wykeham, Bishop of Winchester, after Merton Priory allowed it to decay. The nave windows, south arcade and west tower are of 1888 by W.J.Shearburn.

EGHAM *St John the Baptist* TQ 014714

The present church of 1817-20 by Henry Rhodes contains Royal Arms of Charles II of 1660, a plain 18th century pulpit from Little Livermere in Suffolk, and amongst the monuments are a half-figure of Robert Foster, d1663, a brass to Anthony Bond, d1576 and his two wives, plus a monument with a relief of the first two wives of the Surveyor General, Sir John Denham, Cecile, d1612, and Eleanor. Also from the old church are the 15th century timber porch now used as a lychgate and an inscription recording the rebuilding of the chancel in 1327 by Abbot Rutherwyke of Chertsey.

Brass at East Horsley

Effingham Church

ELSTEAD   *St James*   SU 910436

On the north side of the nave are one 13th century lancet, and two-light windows of the 14th and 15th centuries, while the three-light east window and the timber north porch are 15th century. The tiny chancel is probably Norman or Saxon. There is a king-post roof and a bellcote carried on four posts. The west window and the south aisle and SE vestry are of the thorough restoration of 1871 by Garling.

EPSOM   *St Martin*   TQ 214605

The only medieval parts are the tower with a higher stair turret, and the font, both 15th century. The best of several late 17th century tablets is that to Elizabeth Evelyn, d1691. There are also quite a number of early 19th century monuments. The west front and aisled nave are of 1824 by Charles Hatchard, whilst the crossing, transepts, and chancel on a cathedral scale were begun in 1907 by Sir Charles Nicholson.

ESHER   *St George*   TQ 140646

This church of c1540 is now maintained by the Redundant Churches Fund. It has a wooden bell-turret with a pyramidal roof. The brick south chapel was added in 1725-6 as the family pew of the Duke of Newcastle with arched windows and Corinthian columns and angle-pillars towards the church carrying a pediment. The brick north aisle with a castellated east end was added in 1812. It has an arcade of round oak piers. The monuments include that of Lady Fowler, d1738 and a painted kneeling figure of Lady Lynch, d1702.

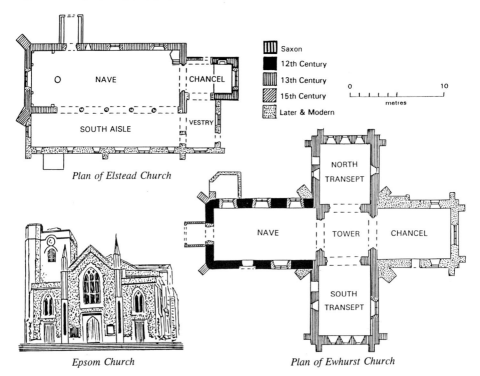

Saxon
12th Century
13th Century
15th Century
Later & Modern

Plan of Elstead Church

Epsom Church

Plan of Ewhurst Church

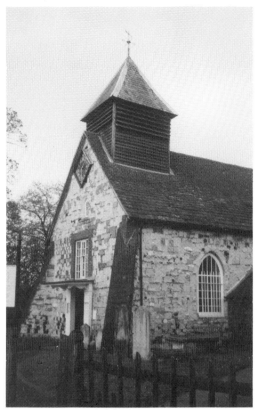

Esher Church   *Ewhurst Church*

EWELL   *St Mary*   TQ 221629

The church of 1848 by Henry Clutton contains a 15th century font with quatrefoil panels, a restored 15th century screen, a wall-monument with a reclining figure of Sir William Lewen, d1721, a kneeling female figure of Mrs Halifax, d1795, and brasses of Lady Iwardby, d1519, Margerina Treglistan, d1521, and Dorothy Taylare, d1577, with her son Edmond Horde, d1575, and his wife.

EWHURST   *St Peter & St Paul*   TQ 092406

The upper parts of the central tower and the chancel are by Robert Ebbels to replace what was destroyed by a collapse of the tower in 1838. The nave has a good Norman south doorway with one order of shafts and two roll-mouldings and a hood-mould coming down onto the imposts. The crossing arches and transepts with triple lancets in their end walls are 13th century. The timber west porch and the large three-light window above it are 15th century. The square font has St Andrew's crosses and chevrons on the sides, and its cover is partly 18th century. The pulpit is Jacobean and the altar rails are late 17th century.

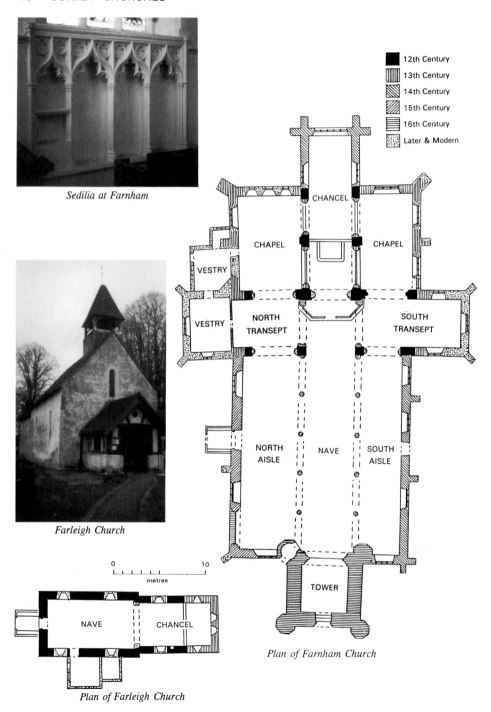

Sedilia at Farnham

Farleigh Church

12th Century
13th Century
14th Century
15th Century
16th Century
Later & Modern

CHANCEL

CHAPEL   CHAPEL

VESTRY

VESTRY   NORTH
TRANSEPT   SOUTH
TRANSEPT

NORTH
AISLE   NAVE   SOUTH
AISLE

0   10
metres

TOWER

Plan of Farnham Church

NAVE   CHANCEL

Plan of Farleigh Church

FARLEIGH *St Mary* TQ 372601

The nave of c1100 has four restored original windows, a west doorway with one order of shafts and a south doorway now opening into a vestry. The chancel is also Norman, but was given two lancets on each side c1250, when it was lengthened, the new east wall having two lancets instead of the usual three. The bell turret has been restored. A brass has small figures of John Brook, d1495, and his wife Anne.

FARNHAM *St Andrew* SU 838466

The Norman church here had a crossing tower and a vaulted chancel of two bays. Of it there remain bits of walling including pilaster buttresses of the chancel visible from the late 12th century chapels, and the west arch of the south chapel re-uses older material. Excavations during a restoration of 1959 revealed the bases of the crossing piers. The south aisle is 14th century, but the reticulated tracery of the windows has been renewed. The wider north aisle dates from a rebuilding after a 15th century fire, when the existing five bay arcades of double-hollow-chamfered arches on octagonal piers were built, and the former crossing given north and south arches to match. The blocked arch at the west end of the north wall led into a former late 15th century Lady chapel. The chapels were given 15th century windows but three lancets have replaced the eastern one of the north chapel. The dedication recorded in 1399 may refer to the extra third bay added to the chancel with ogee-arched sedilia and piscina. The west tower with octagonal corner turrets is 16th century, but the top is of 1865 by Ewan Christian. The ends of the transepts date from the drastic restoration of 1855 by Benjamin Ferrey. The octagonal font with shields and figures is 15th century. The altar rails are late 17th century. The aisle walls are decorated with 18th and 19th century hatchments. There are brasses to Benett Jay, d1586, and his wife Elizabeth, d1594, and Sibil Jay, d1597, There are numerous 18th and 19th century tablets but none of importance.

Farnham Church

Fetcham Church

Farleigh Church

Saxon	
12th Century	14th Century
c1200	15th Century
13th Century	Later & Modern

Plan of Fetcham Church (PORCH, NORTH AISLE, NORTH TRANSEPT, VESTRY, NAVE, CHANCEL, SOUTH AISLE, TOWER)

Plan of Fetcham Church

FETCHAM   *St Mary*   TQ 150556

The late Saxon nave retains one original window with re-used Roman brick above the three bay late 12th century south arcade of chamfered round arches on circular piers. The rectangular south transeptal tower with two original south windows is probably of the end of the 12th century, but the top is mid 18th century. Of the 13th century are the chancel with one north lancet now looking into the vestry, and the north transept with lancets flanking an altar recess with dogtooth ornamentation in the east wall. The transept has a north window of c1325, and the chancel has a 15th century east window. The early 14th century north aisle has an arcade of two very wide bays. The south aisle outer wall has been rebuilt. There is a monument depicting Antony Rous, d1631, as a corpse, and there is a bust of Henry Vincent, d1631.

FRENSHAM   *St Mary*   SU 842414

The diagonally buttressed west tower is probably late 14th century but was restored by Caroe in 1929. The north aisle of 1826 was given a new arcade when the rest of the church was rebuilt in the Decorated style in 1868 to a design by Hahn. One 13th century lancet survives in the chancel and the nave retains a medieval king-post roof. The church contains a huge copper cauldron which is probably 17th century, and a pair of crocketted pinnacles, probably from a destroyed tomb of c1300.

FRIMLEY   *St Peter*   SU 880581

A church of 1825 designed by Parkinson, altered in 1881 by Goodchild, has replaced a timber-framed chapel built in 1606.

GATTON   *St Andrew*   TQ 275529

In 1834 the traveller and art collector Lord Monson had a mostly 15th century church rebuilt except for the east window which now contains foreign glass probably of the late 16th century. A south window contains German glass of c1600. The north transept window with Y-tracery may have been brought in from elsewhere. A covered way connects this part with the house, and it contains a fireplace and padded benches. There is an octagonal 13th century font with five shafts. A 15th century rood screen from another church now supports the west gallery. The nave stalls Baroque work from Ghent, and the panelling there is dated 1515 and came from Aarschot Cathedral in Brabant. Flemish carved scenes of c1530 are incorporated into the altar table and a pulpit which forms part of the gallery front in the south transept. The doors with linenfold patterning in this part are from Rouen. The chancel panelling with linenfold patterning surrounding an original 13th century trefoil piscina is from Burgundy. The late 16th century altar rails are from Tongres in Belgium. The Late Gothic chair also looks Flemish. The medieval lectern is from an unknown source.

Gatton Church

Window at Godalming

Godalming Church

GODALMING   *St Peter & St Paul*   SU 968440

The two blocked double-splayed circular windows in the tower west wall originally lighted a Saxon nave above a chancel arch of that period removed in 1879. The corners of the Saxon chancel still remain, but the outer three walls were pierced with arches when the Normans made it into a central tower with a new chancel beyond and narrow transepts on each side. The tower is now covered by a 13th century lead spire. Traces of the Norman chancel windows remain above the two-bay arcades to the 13th century chapels. The south chapel was lengthened with a fine Geometrical style east window and sedilia in the late 13th century. It has a squint through to the chancel and two 14th century south windows. The chancel east end is 14th century. Aisles were added to the Saxon nave in the 13th century and these were lengthened along with the nave to the west c1400. The west doorway was reset when a fourth bay was added in 1840 and the north chapel was rebuilt. In 1879 the aisles were rebuilt wider and the north transept lengthened. There is also now a SW porch. The Jacobean pulpit has been modified. In the south chapel are a 14th century tomb chest on which lie Saxon carved fragments and brasses to Thomas Purvoche, d1509, and his wife Joan, and John Barker, d1595. The chancel chandelier is of 1722.

GODSTONE   *St Nicholas*   TQ 356515

The north aisle is of the 1840s and the south aisle and much of the rest dates from Sir Giles Gilbert Scott's restoration of 1872-3. Parts of a Norman window remain near the doorway and there is an octagonal 15th century font with pointed quatrefoil panels. There are recumbent effigies of Sir John Evelyn, d1641, and his wife, and there are monuments to James Evelyn, d1793, and Mrs Smith, d1794.

GREAT BOOKHAM   *St Nicholas*   TQ 135546

The late 12th century four-bay north arcade of chamfered pointed arches on octagonal columns was blocked up when the aisle was removed but the three eastern arches were re-opened for a new aisle added in 1844-5 by Robert Carpenter. The mid 12th century south arcade has round arches on circular columns with square capitals. The west end of the south aisle retains its original narrow width and a tiny west window but the rest, and the former 14th century two storey south porch, have been absorbed into the 15th century Slyfield chapel which is twice the width. The chancel of 1341 has reticulated tracery in the three-light east window and cusped Y-tracery in the side windows. Beyond a Victorian north vestry is a large extension of 1923. The west tower is timber-framed but has a flint bottom stage of c1200. The 15th century stained glass in the east window is Flemish or German work brought here from Costessey Hall in Norfolk. There are brasses to Elizabeth Slyfield, d1443, Henry Slyfield, d1598, and his wife Elizabeth, and Robert Shiers, d1668, in the dress of a bencher of the Inner Temple. There are busts of Robert Shiers, d1668, and his wife Elizabeth, d1700, and his son George, d1685. There is also an effigy in Roman dress of Arthur Moore, d1735.

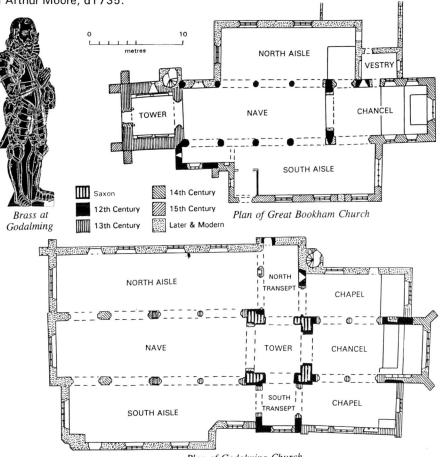

Brass at Godalming

0   10
metres

	Saxon		14th Century
	12th Century		15th Century
	13th Century		Later & Modern

NORTH AISLE

VESTRY

TOWER

NAVE

CHANCEL

SOUTH AISLE

Plan of Great Bookham Church

NORTH AISLE

NORTH TRANSEPT

CHAPEL

NAVE

TOWER

CHANCEL

SOUTH TRANSEPT

CHAPEL

SOUTH AISLE

Plan of Godalming Church

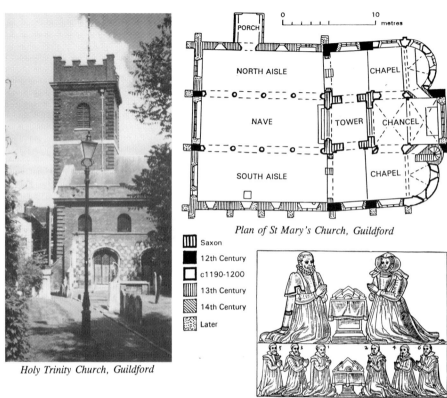

Holy Trinity Church, Guildford

Plan of St Mary's Church, Guildford

||| Saxon
■ 12th Century
☐ c1190-1200
|||| 13th Century
⧄ 14th Century
▦ Later

Brass at Holy Trinity Church, Guildford

GUILDFORD   *Holy Trinity*   SU 998494

After the tower collapsed the church was rebuilt in 1749-63 by James Horne, except for the chapel at the west end of the south side which contained the Weston Chantry founded in 1540. The 18th century work has brick quoins, five bays of round headed windows (in two tiers until altered by Woodyer in 1869), a pedimented west end and an embattled west tower. The interior was remodelled when Sir Arthur Blomfield added a chancel and apse in 1888, so only the west gallery is original. The pulpit is of c1770, although it looks older. Under the tower is a reclining effigy of Sir Robert Parkhurst, d1637, and an effigy of an un-named female, probably slightly earlier. In the nave is a semi-reclining effigy in Roman dress of Arthur Onslow, d1778, Speaker of the House of Commons for 33 years, and a monument to James Smyth, d1711. In the transept is a monument with a six-columned canopy and effigy of Archbishop George Abbot, d1633. There is also a brass to his parents, Maurice and Alice, who both died in 1606, and another brass depicts a civilian of c1500.

GUILDFORD   *St Catherine*   SU 994475

High above the water meadows of the Wey is a ruined single chamber of c1300. It has big buttresses intended to carry pinnacles which divide it into three bays and there is a polygonal NW corner stair turret. No tracery survives in the windows, which were of two lights in the side walls, and of three lights in the east wall.

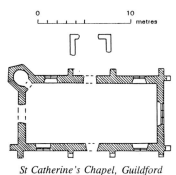

St Catherine's Chapel, Guildford

St Catherine's, Guildford

GUILDFORD   *St Mary*   SU 996493

The central tower is Late Saxon work with narrow pilaster strips and double-splayed windows visible under the roofs. The nave, chancel, and transepts are early 12th century and the north and south arches of the tower are of that date. In the 1180s the church was remodelled with aisles with four bay arcades of pointed arches on round piers, the chancel was given an apse, a rare feature at this late date, and the transepts were extended eastward into apsidal ended chapels. These side apses with their vaults and lancets still remain but the central apse was removed in 1825 to allow the road beyond to be widened. In the early 13th century the chancel was rib-vaulted in two bays and given squints through from the apses, and then a little later the aisles were rebuilt much wider. The external details (including several late medieval windows) were mostly renewed in 1862 by Thomas Goodchild but the north doorway is 13th century work and the interior remains intact and is characterised by a big rise in floor level up to the east with many steps. Hardly anything now remains of original wall-paintings in the north apse recorded in the 19th century. The organ case incorporates part of a 15th century reredos. The only monument of interest is a brass of a civilian and wife of c1500 in the north chapel.

Interior of St Mary's Church, Guildford.

North apse, St Mary's Church, Guildford

*Brasses at
St Mary's Guildford*

GUILDFORD   *St Nicholas*   SU 994494

Much of this church, which has an apse and central tower, dates from a rebuilding of 1870-5 by Teulon but some 15th century work remains in the Loseley chapel on the south side. It contains a damaged recumbent effigy of Arnold Brocas, rector in 1395, recumbent effigies of Sir William More, d1600, and his wife, two monuments of the same period with kneeling effigies and several 17th and 18th century tablets. In the south aisle is a cartouche of James Knowles, d1741, and in the porch is a brass to Caleb Lovejoy, d1676.

HASCOMBE   *St Peter*   TQ 002395

The fine church of 1864 by Henry Woodyer contains a square font of 1690 and a tablet to William Middlefield, d1785.

HASLEMERE   *St Bartholomew*

SU 904334

The church was entirely rebuilt in 1870 except for the 13th century tower with a 17th century top stage. The oldest monument is to Captain Charles Lydiard, d1807. The west window contains a pair of 17th century Flemish stained glass panels.

HEADLEY   *St Mary*   TQ 205548

In the vestry of the church of 1855 by Salvin with a tower of 1859 by Street lie two painted tablets to Elizabeth Leate, d1680, and Margaret Warren, d1675.

HORLEY   *St Bartholomew*

TQ 276428

The north aisle was probably built after the church was appropriated by Chertsey Abbey in 1313. Until the church was heavily restored in 1881 by Arthur Blomfield the aisle windows had Kentish tracery. Original are the arcade and the north doorway and porch. Also 14th century are the arch between the chancel and north chapel for a effigy of a knight of the Salaman family with a lion at his feet. Standing on four posts within the aisle is a tower of the same date. The shingling of the bell-stage and spire is 16th or 17th century. In the chancel are brasses of a lady of c1420 under a canopy with thin shafts and a man in civilian dress of c1510.

St Mary's Church, Guildford

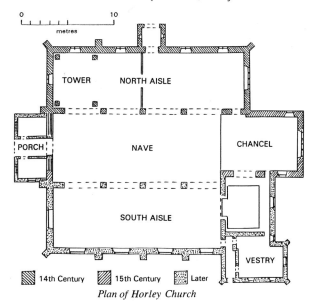

Plan of Horley Church

HORNE   *St Mary*   TQ 336444

The church was much altered and restored by Gordon Mills in 1880. He used two columns from the former west gallery to support a new porch. Of the 15th century are the font, a screen now at the west end and a windows in the north aisle. On the south side there is also a 14th century window. The chancel inclines to the north. There are small kneeling effigies of John Goodwine, d1618, and his wife.

HORSELL   *St Mary*   SU 994593

The diagonally buttressed west tower and the south aisle and arcade are 15th century. The rest is mostly restored or rebuilt. There are kneeling effigies of James Fenn, d1787, and his wife, and brasses to John Sutton, d1603, Thomas Sutton, d1603, and Thomas Edmonds, d1619, and his wife Ann.

KEW   *St Anne*   TQ 190775

In 1770 J.J.Kirby lengthened the church of 1710-4 of yellow brick with arched red brick windows and added a north aisle. The west front was built by Sir Jeffry Wyatville in 1836. The mausoleum of the Duke and Duchess of Cambridge at the east end was added in 1850-1 to a design by Benjamin Ferrey. In 1884 Henry Stock added a south aisle and provided five-bay arcades with wooden Tuscan columns and a vaulted ceiling. There are white and gold columns in the apse and pink scagliola columns under the crossing, whilst the dome on squinches has gold stars on a blue background. The only pre-Victorian monument is that of Lady Capel, d1721.

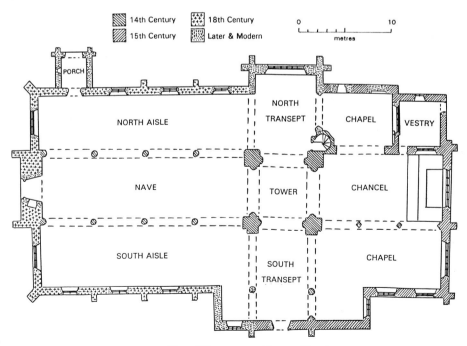

Plan of Kington-upon-Thames Church

Kew Church

KINGSTON-UPON-THAMES

All Saints   TQ 179693

A Norman west doorway was destroyed during Robert Brandon's restoration of 1862-6. This campaign, plus another in 1883 by Pearson are responsible for all the windows, the north porch, much of the north transept and the west aisle of the south transept. The four bay arcades are of c1400 but the walls of the wide aisles are 18th century. The arches of the central tower are of c1300 and it has a brick top of 1708. The chancel with a three bay arcade to St James' chapel on the south and a single arch to Holy Trinity chapel on the north, plus the NE vestry are all 15th century, the arcade piers being of a four-shafts-four-hollows section. The font is late 17th century. There is a fragment of a Saxon cross-shaft with interlace. There are brasses to Robert Skerne, d1437, and his wife Joan, and John Hertcombe, d1488, and his wife Katherine. Other monuments include a 15th century tomb chest in the south chapel, a recumbent effigy of Sir Anthony Benn, d1618, and memorials to Henry Davidson, d1781, by Regnart, and Philip Meadows, made by Flaxman in 1795.

Kington-upon-Thames Church

LALEHAM   *All Saints*   TQ 052689

The exterior is restored or rebuilt except for the brick west tower dated 1732 and the Lucan chapel of c1500 on the north side with brick diaper-work. Inside are Norman arches of single-chamfered arches on round columns. The south aisle has been removed and the arcade blocked up. Reset on this side are parts of a former Norman doorway. Monuments in the chancel include those of George Perrot, d1780, and his wife, d1784, both by William Tyler.

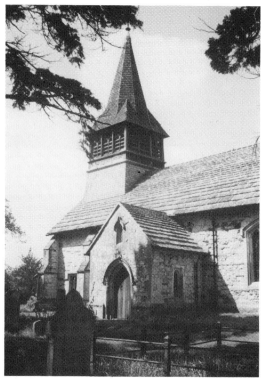

Leigh Church   *Leatherhead Church*

LEATHERHEAD   *St Mary & St Nicholas*   TQ 168561

The church has a very irregular layout with the 14th century chancel and transepts inclined to the north from the axis of the Norman nave, whilst the 15th century west tower with angle buttresses and a NE stair-turret is quite dramatically inclined to the south. The aisle walls and north porch are 15th century although most of the external details have been restored and the northern part of the north transept has been rebuilt. The four bay arcades of the early 13th century have pointed arches with the inner order chamfered and piers alternately round and octagonal. The SW arch is narrower than the others and the NW arch is Victorian. The chancel has a blocked NE doorway to a destroyed contemporary vestry. The octagonal font with quatrefoils is 15th century. The leather-bound chest with stud patterns is dated 1663. The north aisle windows have jumbled fragments of medieval glass. There are monuments to Richard Dalton, d1731, and Jacob Wishart, d1723, and a brass of a man of c1470.

LEIGH   *St Bartholomew*   TQ 224470

The bellcote and west end are of 1890 by F.C.Less in replacement of a tower added in 1856 to a small late medieval church. A new font bowl sits on the nine columns and base of the old one, whose damaged original bowl lies nearby. Under a carpet in the chancel are brasses of John Arderne, d1449, his wife Elizabeth, and daughter Susan, and a Trinity from the brass of Richard Arderne, d1499, and his wife Joan.

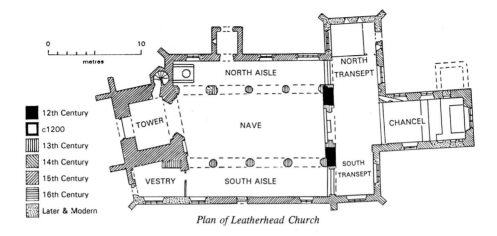

12th Century
c1200
13th Century
14th Century
15th Century
16th Century
Later & Modern

Plan of Leatherhead Church

LIMPSFIELD   *St Peter*   TQ 405534

The nave west wall has Norman herringbone masonry. Of the 13th century are the south aisle with a three bay arcade of slightly chamfered arches on circular piers, the chancel with south lancets and the north chapel with a two bay arcade between these parts. South of the chancel is a tower of c1180 with a plain arch towards the chancel, a pyramidal roof, and a south window with plate tracery of c1260. A similar east window was moved from the tower to a vestry in 1823, but was destroyed in the restoration of 1871, when many of the windows were renewed. The south porch is 16th century. The north aisle was added in 1852. The square font with corner shafts is 13th century. There is a monument to Marmaduke Hilton, d1768.

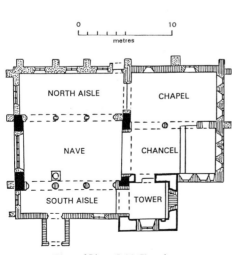

Plan of Limpsfield Church

Limpsfield Church

Lingfield Church

Littleton Church

LINGFIELD   *St Peter & St Paul*   TQ 389438

Apart from a 14th century tower at the SW end of the nave the whole church dates from the two decades after Sir Reginald Cobham founded a college at Lingfield in 1431. The church is quite spacious and has a two bay south aisle, a four bay north aisle and a three bay chancel flanked by north and south chapels. The nave piers have four shafts and four hollows, whilst the chapel arcade piers have a more complex section. The north side has a sequence of three-light windows under segmental hood-moulds only broken by the rood-staircase turret. There are larger windows of four and five lights at the east and west ends.

Lingfield has the best set of medieval furnishings in Surrey and a good selection of monuments. There are original screens closing off the chapels from the chancel and there are stalls with miserichords with the usual motifs of angels bearing shields. The octagonal font has an original ogival shaped cover. The wooden lectern may also be medieval. Of the 18th century are the chandelier and the Royal Arms of Queen Anne. The bench on the north side of the chancel with a figure in 16th century armour probably originally formed a chimneypiece in a house. In the chancel are brasses of the priests John Wyche, d1445, John Swetcote, d1469, James Veldon, d1458, John Knoyll, d1508, and of a young girl of c1450, effigies of Sir Reginald Cobham, d1446, and his wife, and two Baroque cartouches to Francis Howard, d1695, and his wife Mary, d1718. The north chapel contains an effigy of Reginald, 1st Lord Cobham, d1361 on an embattled tomb chest, an altar tomb possibly of Sir Thomas Cobham, d1471, and brasses to Reginald, 2nd Lord Cobham, d1403, Eleanor (first wife of Sir Reginald), d1420, with a canopy and marginal inscription, a small figure of Katherine Stoket, d1420, a brass of John Hadresham, d1417, and a fine brass possibly of Elizabeth (second wife of Sir Reginald), d1375. There is also an unusual incised effigy of c1530 made up from encaustic tiles, a foreign import.

Brass at Lingfield

Little Bookham Church

LITTLE BOOKHAM   *Dedication Unknown*   TQ 124541

With the demolition of the south aisle and the blocking of the Norman arcade of round arches on circular piers with square capitals, the church is reduced to a single main chamber with a 13th century east end and a 19th century vestry and organ chamber on the north side. Norman windows survive in the west wall and at the west end of the north wall. In the blocked arches are a reset 15th century window and a renewed 13th century lancet. The Norman font has 17th century iron straps.

LITTLETON   *St Mary Magdalene*   TQ 071687

The 13th century chancel is longer than the contemporary nave. Brick additions are the early 16th century south porch, nave clerestory, and west tower heightened in the 18th century, plus the north chapel dated 1705 with chequerwork and a double-curved gable, soon afterwards extended further north. The south aisle was refaced in the 19th century. The arcades of c1200 on the south with a round pier and of the late 13th century with an octagonal pier on the north have double-chamfered arches. All late medieval are the restored pews and rood screen, the choir stalls, and the locker in the south wall. The altar rails are Flemish or French Baroque of c1700. The pulpit is early 18th century.

LONG DITTON   *St Mary*   TQ 173660

Brasses of Robert Castleton, d1527, and his wife Elizabeth, and Richard Hatton, d1616, and his wife Mary lie in G.E.Street's church of 1878-80 which replaced a building of 1776 by Sir Robert Taylor in the form of a Greek cross, the floor and wall stumps of which remain in the churchyard. Loose architectural fragments at the west end are all that remain of the medieval church on this site.

MALDON   *St John*   TQ 211663

The medieval chancel and the nave and tower erected by John Goode, d1627 (see the inscription on the east wall) were restored in 1863 by T.G.Jackson. In 1875 the nave and chancel became the south aisle and south chapel of a new church erected to the north by the same architect.

MERROW   *St John*   TQ 028508

The only features to survive a rebuilding of 1842 by R.C.Hussey and the addition of a north aisle in 1881 by Sir A.W.Blomfield are the south arcade of c1200, what was probably once a chancel arch of c1200 now set on new responds at the east end of the aisle, and the arch of the north doorway with chevrons ornamentation of c1150.

MERSTHAM   *St Katharine*   TQ 290538

The west tower with a fine west doorway with nook-shafts and an order of dog-tooth mouldings is of c1220. There are lancets in the bell-chamber and a shingled broach-spire. Also 13th century are the aisles with arcades of three bays with circular piers on the south and octagonal ones on the north, the clerestory of quatrefoils and trefoils, the chancel arch and the walling of the chancel with remains of large scale blank arcading inside, plus the square font with corner shafts. The south porch and five-light east window are 15th century and the north and south chapels are of c1500. Each has an arcade with a narrow west bay and a wider east bay. The remains of a frieze with foliage and half-figures in the north chapel are from a tomb recess or parclose screen. This chapel contains a tomb chest with brasses of the wives of John Elingbridge, d1473 (his own figure is missing), and a brass to John Newdegate, d1498, and in the north aisle is a damaged 15th century effigy. In the chancel are brasses to John Ballard, d1463, and his wife Margaret and Thomas Elmerugge, d1507 and his wife Joan. A brass in the south aisle depicts the sons of Nicholas and Elizabeth Best, Peter, d1585, being shown in swaddling clothes, whilst Richard, d1587, is shown as a young boy. The tablet to Lieutenant George Jolliffe, who was killed at the battle of the Nile in 1797, has a relief depicting the battle.

Mickleham Church

Merstham Church

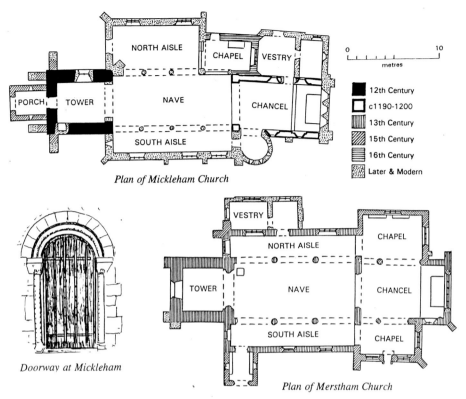

Plan of Mickleham Church

Doorway at Mickleham

Plan of Merstham Church

MERTON *St Mary*   TQ 252694

The Norman nave retains a rebuilt north doorway with chevrons and original ironwork on the door. One Norman window survives west of the north aisle added in 1866. The early 13th century chancel has blocked north windows in four bays of blank internal arcading and a later hammer-beam roof. The bells are contained in a broach-spire perched on the nave roof. There is a 15th century timber north porch. A south aisle was added in 1856. A wall monument has kneeling effigies of Gregory Lovell, d1597 and his wives. Captain Cook's wife erected a monument to the Smith family. The fine doorway of c1175 re-erected in the churchyard is a relic of Merton Priory.

MICKLEHAM *St Michael*   TQ 171534

The Norman west tower has later set-back corner buttresses and a broached spike on the truncated top. The west doorway has one order of shafts with scallop capitals and roll-moulding. The Late Norman chancel has two original windows on each side, those on the north now looking into vestries, and the chancel arch has diamond and dog-tooth mouldings on the outer order. The Norbury chapel on the north side with chequerboarding of flint and clunch contains a tomb chest with brasses of William Wyddowson, d1515, and his wife Joan. In 1871 a wide three-bay north aisle was added, plus a narrow four-bay south aisle and a round turret to contain the organ, whilst the east wall was also rebuilt. There is a Belgian pulpit of c1600 with scenes in panels and saints under corner crockets. The Norman font has arcading.

Morden Church

MITCHAM   *St Peter & St Paul*   TQ 271687

The large church is of 1819-21 except for the medieval south transeptal tower. There are portrait memorials to Sir Ambrose Crowley, d1713, and Lady Crowley, d1727. The best of several late 18th century tablets is that to Sophia Tata, d1780.

MORDEN   *St Lawrence*   TQ 250675

This is a brick single chamber of 1636, although possibly a refacing of an older structure. It has stone quoins, late medieval style windows, an embattled west tower and a south porch. The roof has tie-beams and king-posts. Of 1720 are the pulpit and test and the three-sided altar rail. There are tablets of the 1770s to two Lehups.

MORTLAKE   *St Mary*   TQ 208760

The west tower dates from 1543, when Henry VIII had the church moved from its original position. The font could possibly be slightly earlier. The top stage of the tower is of 1694 and the open lantern dates from 1815, the period of the nave north wall with round-arched windows. Otherwise the nave was rebuilt in 1905 and the chancel is of 1885, the work being overseen by Sir Arthur Blomfield. The arch in the churchyard contains material from the original tower doorway. The oldest monuments are to Francis Coventry, d1699, and Nicholas Godschall, d1748.

Newdigate Church

NEWDIGATE   *St Peter*   TQ 198422

A two-light window of c1260 dates the chancel. It also has several lancets but the east window is of 1876-7. The south aisle with a piscina and east window with ogee-headed lights and an arcade with double-chamfered arches on a round pier with octagonal capitals is 14th century. The north aisle of 1877 has a similar arcade and one window there has fragments of reset 14th century glass. The timber-framed belfry with diagonal cross-bracing between the posts is 15th century. There is a brass inscription to Joane Smallpiece, d1634.

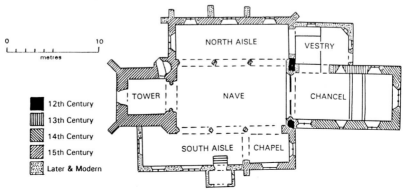

Plan of Nutfield Church

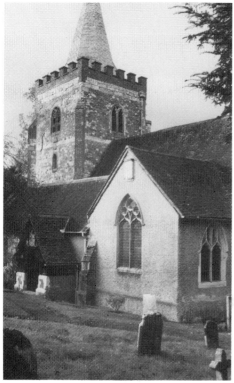

Nutfield Church

Ockham Church

NUTFIELD   *St Peter & St Paul*   TQ 309509

The 13th century chancel has one lancet on each side, that on the north now looking into a vestry which has replaced a chantry chapel. Of the 15th century are the diagonal buttressed west tower with a NE stair turret and brick top of 1786, the walls of the north aisle and the south transeptal chapel and the chancel SW window. The features were almost all renewed in 1882 by William Milne and the south chapel then absorbed into a new south aisle with a porch covering the reset doorway. The font has an octagonal 15th century bowl on a stem dated 1665. The much restored screen may be 14th century. In the chancel are brasses of William Grafton, c1465, and his wife Joan and a monument probably to Thomas de Pulham, rector 1305-28.

OAKWOOD   *St John the Baptist*   TQ 128380

The church has a delightful setting alone in woods with only the church hall nearby. It was a 13th century single chamber founded as a chapel-of-ease to Wotton and had lancets on both sides until in 1879 Basil Champneys added a north aisle. He reset in it the doorway, aumbry and four lancets from the original north wall replaced by a three bay arcade to the nave with a further two bays to the chancel. An original priest's doorway on the south now opens into a vestry. The 15th century west doorway has a drawbar slot. There is a brass to Edward de la Hale, d1431.

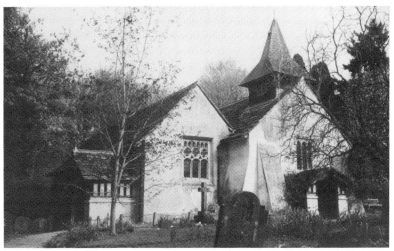

Oakwood Church

OCKHAM *All Saints* TQ 066566

The set of seven lancets in the east wall of the chancel is equalled only at Blakeney in Norfolk and Kilkenny Friary in Ireland. It dates from c1260 and was probably transferred here from nearby Newark Priory since it has a rere-arch which looks 16th century and below it outside are the stumps of three more widely-spaced lancets. The chancel arch and north arcade of two double-chamfered arches are probably early 13th century. The nave south wall, with a pair of three-light windows containing German 18th century glass, is 14th century. One chancel south window has fragments of 15th century glass. The aisle was rebuilt in the 15th century when a diagonally buttressed west tower with a SE stair-turret was added. The nave wagon roof with bosses and diamond-patterned panels is of c1530 and there is a similar roof in the aisle. The north chapel, although mostly rebuilt, contains a fine canopied 14th century niche. Beyond the north aisle is a brick chapel built to contain the tomb with effigies of Peter, 1st Lord King, d1734, and his wife, made by Rysbrack. Beside the high altar are brasses of the priest Walter Frilende, d1376, (the earliest of this type in Surrey) and John Weston, d1483, and his wife Margaret, d1475.

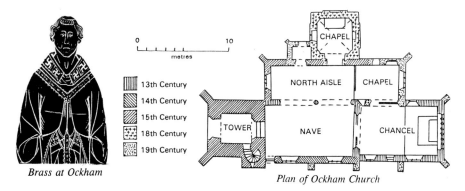

13th Century
14th Century
15th Century
18th Century
19th Century

Brass at Ockham

Plan of Ockham Church

OCKLEY   *St Margaret*   TQ 156406

The chancel was rebuilt in 1873 but retains some old masonry. A new aisle was then
also added. The nave south wall has two windows and a doorway of the 14th
century. The west tower was rebuilt in 1699 but the doorway at the foot of the NE
stair-turret looks medieval and inside are four old-looking arches suggesting the rather
unlikely scenario that c1200 this was a central tower of a cruciform church. There
is a timber 15th century west porch.

OLD WOKING   *St Peter*   TQ 021561

The nave north wall is Norman and the chancel and lower part of the tower with
angle buttresses are 13th century. Of the 15th century are the tower top, the south
aisle and arcade, and the nave north windows. The nave west doorway is a fine piece
of c1100 complete with the original door with its ornamental ironwork. The west
gallery is of 1622 and the pulpit is of about the same period. There are late medieval
pews with narrow buttresses at the ends. In the south aisle are brasses of John
Shadhet, d1527, and his wife Isabel, and a figure of Joan Purdan of the same period,
also once part of a family group. There are tablets to Johannes Lloyd, d1663, John
Merest, d1752, and the Reverend Edward Emily, d1792.

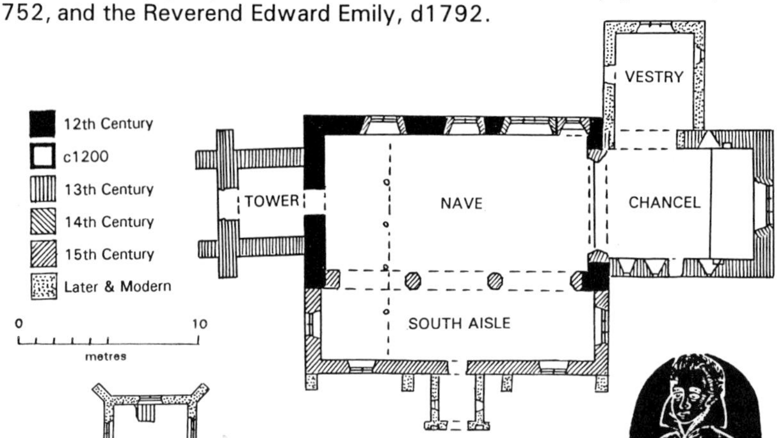

Plan of Old Woking Church

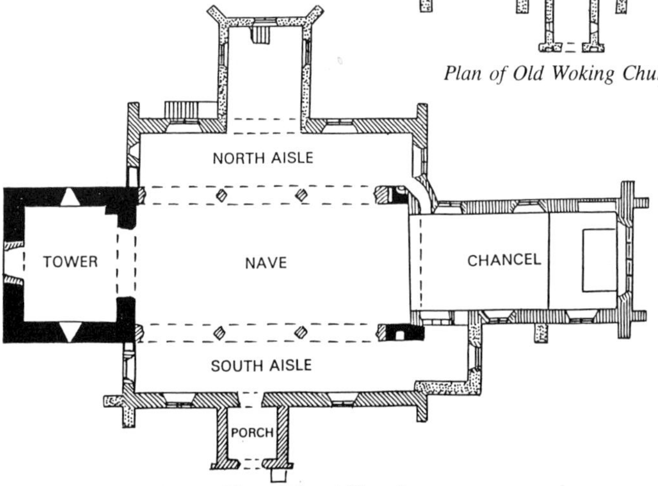

Plan of Oxted Church

Brass at Oxted

Old Woking Church

OXTED *St Mary* TQ 391530

The low west tower is Norman. The chancel is 13th century although the only feature of that period is the priest's door now opening into the organ chamber. The windows are 14th century, as are the aisles, but only the north aisle east window has survived restoration. The south porch with the Cobham arms in the spandrels of the outer arch, and the arcades of three bays with piers of four-shafts-and-four-hollows section are 15th century. A few traces remain of the original lower 13th century aisles and their arcades. The iron chest is 15th century. The east window contains 14th century glass showing the four evangelists. In the chancel are a brass to Johanne Haselden, d1480, kneeling figures of John Aldersley, d1610, and his wife, part of a brass to the priest John Ynge, d1428, a brass to three of Sir Thomas Hoskins' sons, Thomas and Thomas, d1611, and John, d1618, plus a tablet to William Finch, d1728.

Ockley Church

Pirbright Church

Petersham Church   *Brass at Peper Harrow*

PEPER HAROW   *St Nicholas*   SU 934440

The nave south wall contains a Norman south doorway and an ogival-headed 14th century lancet. The west tower is of 1826 but the tower arch, north aisle, chancel windows and the mortuary chapel are all of 1844 by Pugin. He made the chancel arch neo-Norman, presumably because traces of an original Norman chancel arch then still existed. There is a brass of 1487 to Joan Adderley, who also has a brass cross and inscription on the chancel floor. There is also a tiny brass to young Elizabeth Woodes, d1624, and the chancel contains one 18th century tablet. Brought here in 1900 from All Saints' church at Wandsworth is a monument probably by Bushnell with very fine busts of Sir Thomas Broderick, d1641, and his wife, d1678.

PETERSHAM   *St Peter*   TQ 182734

The 13th century chancel has a blocked north lancet. The red brick nave and embattled west tower with an octagonal lantern are probably 17th century. The nave is dwarfed by a huge 18th century north transept and an equally large south transept of 1840. The interior has mostly 18th and early 19th century furnishings with galleries, box pews, a two-decker pulpit with an iron handrail to the steps, and a font signed John Long fecit 1797. There are reclining 17th century effigies of George Cole, and his wife and namesake grandson.

PIRBRIGHT   *St Michael*   SU 943559

The stone tower is dated 1785 and the nave of red and grey brick is of the same period. The mortar-joints of the tower walls are galletted with tiny dark pebbles. The chancel was remodelled in the 19th century. The arcade inside has Doric piers carrying lintels, and there is an L-shaped gallery.

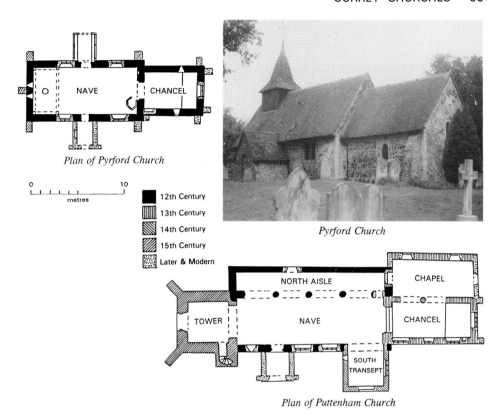

Plan of Pyrford Church

0 ⌊ _ _ _ _ _ ⌋ 10
metres

■ 12th Century
▥ 13th Century
▨ 14th Century
▧ 15th Century
▦ Later & Modern

Pyrford Church

Plan of Puttenham Church

PUTTENHAM   *St John the Baptist*   SU 934478

Of the late 12th century are the south doorway with one order of shafts with scalloped capitals and the four bay arcade of plain round arches on circular piers with square scalloped capitals. The narrow aisle has no features other than a 19th century doorway. The chancel and the north chapel are 13th century with two plain arches between them, although much of the chapel was rebuilt in brick in 1770. The south transept is 14th century and the diagonally buttressed west tower with a SE stair-turret is 15th century. Most of the windows were renewed in a restoration by Henry Woodyer, who added the south porch and the triangular dormer windows on the north side. There is a brass to Rector Edward Cranford, d1431.

PYRFORD   *St Nicholas*   TQ 040582

The nave and chancel are both Norman with an original narrow arch of two orders between them. The chancel has one original north window and the nave two doorways, that on the north having chevrons on the arch and nook-shafts, whilst two Norman windows in the west wall flank a 15th century central buttress. This end has posts carrying a shingled bell-turret with a broach-spire. The east window with some original stained glass is 14th century and the timber north porch is 16th century. The nave south wall has wall paintings of c1200 showing the Flagellation, horsemen and a procession of men with staves. The pulpit is dated 1628.

Ripley Church

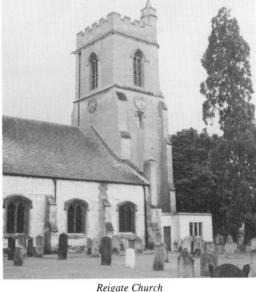

Reigate Church

REIGATE   *St Mary*   TQ 259502

In the early 14th century the original four bay arcades of c1200 with piers round, octagonal and quatrefoil shaped (and out of line with each other on each side), were lengthened by adding a fifth bay (and replacing the easternmost arch on the north side) A new chancel was then added with north and south chapels and ogival-headed sedilia and piscina. The two bay arcades of the chapels, the aisle outer walls with a south porch, and the angle-buttressed west tower are all 15th century, but the external details are mostly of Henry Woodyer's restoration of 1845, whilst the younger George Gilbert Scott refaced the tower in Bath stone in 1877-81. The two storey vestry beyond the north chapel was added c1513. One reset late 13th century window remains in the north aisle west wall. The heavily restored screen is 15th century. Little of the 14th century reredos survived restoration in 1845. There is a stone with a portion of Saxon interlace ornamentation. There are effigies of Sir Thomas Bludden, d1618, and his wife, Richard Elyot, d1608, and his wife, Kathleen Elyot, d1623, Richard Ladbroke, d1730, shown reclining in Roman dress, whilst there are several 18th century cartouches too high up in the tower to be seen properly.

RICHMOND   *St Mary Magdalene*   TQ 179748

The only medieval feature is the west tower of c1500. The nave of yellow and red brick of 1750 has a pediment over the three middle windows on the south and until it was removed in 1824 this was balanced on the north side by a porch. The stone chancel was added in 1904 by G.F.Bodley. Inside are arcades of five bays with slim Tuscan columns and a roof of 1866. The pulpit and font are 18th century. A brass plate has kneeling figures of Robert Cotton, d1591, and his wife Grace. There are busts of John Bently, d1660, and William Rowan, d1767. Other monuments include those of Victor Brounkey of Castle Lyons, d1688, Sophia, widow of Sir Richard Chaworth, d1689, Randolph Greenway, d1754, and Frances Lascelles, d1761.

Reigate Church

RIPLEY *St Mary* TQ 052567

The Norman chancel with clasping buttresses and north windows nook-shafted on the inside has piers in the corners and in the middle of the sides for an intended rib-vault of two bays. The south side has two 13th century lancets and there are three in the east wall. The nave is of 1846 by Benjamin Ferrey and the aisle was added in 1869 by Thomas Jackson.

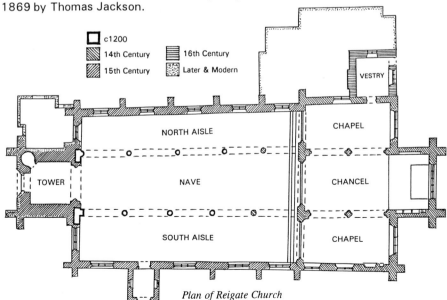

Plan of Reigate Church

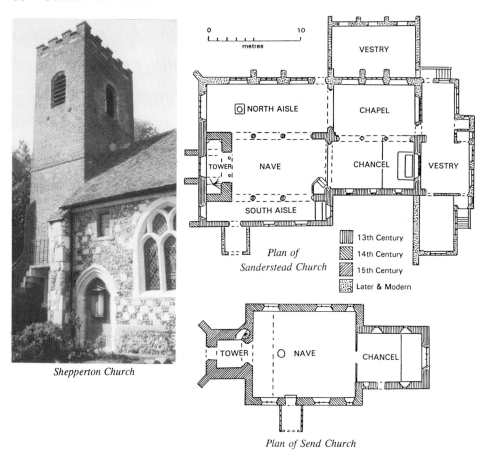

Shepperton Church

VESTRY

NORTH AISLE

CHAPEL

TOWER

NAVE

CHANCEL

VESTRY

SOUTH AISLE

*Plan of
Sanderstead Church*

	13th Century
	14th Century
	15th Century
	Later & Modern

TOWER

NAVE

CHANCEL

Plan of Send Church

SANDERSTEAD   *All Saints*   TQ 342614

The bell-turret is supported by an oblong 14th century bay flanked by the aisles and cutting into the westernmost arches of the three bay 13th century arcades with double-chamfered arches on octagonal piers. The chancel is 13th century but has windows of 1832. On either side of the east window are 14th century painted figures of King Edmund and an archbishop. Over the chancel arch are painted Royal Arms of Charles I. There are brasses of John Awodde, d1525, and his wife Dyones, and there is a kneeling effigy of John Ownstead, d1600. Mary Audley, d1655 has a recumbent effigy bundled in a burial shroud with only the face visible. The tablet and bust of c1730 at the west end of the north aisle are probably to the son of Henry Mellish.

SEALE   *Dedication Unknown*   SU 897479

The church has a central tower with a pyramidal spire but was mostly rebuilt in 1861-73 by Croft. The timber south porch is the chief surviving medieval feature. There is a Rococo tablet to Anne Woodroffe, d1762. The naval accident that killed Edward Noel Long in 1809 is depicted in a relief on his monument.

Brass at Sanderstead

Sanderstead Church

SEND *St Mary* TQ 018543

The 13th century chancel has lancets on the north and south sides and others, now blocked, in the east wall in which is a window of 1819. The timber south porch and the west tower are all 15th century, although the tower bell-openings are Late Georgian. The wide unaisled nave is late 14th century with pairs of three-light windows on each side, plus narrower ones which light the much restored screen. There are trussed beams instead of a chancel arch. The west gallery is late 17th century. A brass has small figures of Laurence Slyfield, d1521, and his wife Alice.

SHALFORD *St Mary* SU 999478

The present church of 1846 by Benjamin Ferrey replaces a classical style church of 1790 from which have come several 18th century tablets, including those of Robert Austen, d1759, and Robert Austen, d1797, by Moorhouse and Bacon respectively.

SHEPPERTON *St Nicholas* TQ 077666

This is a cruciform church mostly of 1614 although the south wall and south transept incorporate medieval masonry and there is a 13th century font. There are wooden early 19th century box pews and galleries at the west ends of the nave and north transept. The oblong brick tower is of 1710.

Interior of Shere Church

Brass at Shere

Plan of Shere Church

■ 12th Century

□ c1200

▦ 13th Century

▨ 14th Century

▒ Later & Modern

SHERE   *St James*   TQ 074478

The Norman tower has a two-light window on the north side and single bell-openings. It carries a large broach-spire. Also Norman are a window high up in the south transept west wall and the two orders of chevrons forming part of a south doorway of 1200, built as part of a new aisle and south chapel. The south arcade has been altered but one arch of that period remains on the north side. The south chapel was lengthened c1300 and the chancel was extended shortly afterwards and has an ogee arch in its east window and a quatrefoil window and squint on the north. The north window of the shortened north transept is mid 14th century. One south window has a brass inscription and effigy of its donor Oliver Sandes, d1512. Old roofs, mostly of the scissors-truss type, survived the restoration of 1895 by S. Weatherley, when the vestry was added. The font of c1200 has a bowl with three scallops on each side supported on a central stem and four corner-shafts with still-leaf capitals. The aisle east window and several others have fragments of 14th century glass. There is a small brass to Rector Robert Scarclyf, d1412. Other brasses show John Redford, d1516 and his wife, and young woman of c1520. Only the top half of the brass of c1525 to John Towchet, Lord Audley, d1490, is original, the rest being of 1911.

STAINES *St Mary* TQ 031719

The two lower stages of the brick west tower are of c1630. The top stage was built in 1828 when the church was rebuilt in yellow stock-brick with lancet windows. The east apse is of 1885. Inside is a gallery with an iron balustrade on three sides.

STANWELL *St Mary* TQ 056742

The lowest stage of the west tower and the south arcade with circular and octagonal piers are 13th century. The next stage of the tower, the aisle east window, and the side windows of the chancel are early 14th century. The chancel also has sedilia with many ogees of that date and its trussed-rafter roof may be of that period. The top stage of the tower and the shingled spire are late 14th century, and the clerestory and nave roof are 15th century. Only the corbels carved with a queen, two kings, a bishop, a knight, a man, a woman, and pilgrim remain of the 14th century aisle roof. There is a Norman pillar piscina. There are large kneeling figures of Lord and Lady Knyvett, d1622, by Nicholas Stone, and in the chancel is a brass with a half figure of Richard de Thorp, d1408.

STOKE *St John the Evangelist* SU 998508

Much of the church is of the restoration of 1858 by Thomas Goodchild and there is a large modern vestry complex on the south side. Medieval parts are the much restored 15th century west tower with a tall chequerboarded stair turret, the 15th century east window of five lights, and the 14th century arcades of the chancel chapels, with double-chamfered arches on the north side, but more complex moulded arches on the south. The north chapel has 17th century mullion-and-transom windows. The black marble font is 18th century. The north chapel east window has old heraldic stained glass. The oldest of the many memorial tablets are to Henry and William Parson, d1799, and William Aldersey, d1800.

Stanwell Church

Stoke Church

STOKE D'ABERNON   *St Mary*   TQ 129584

The nave and the chancel inclined to the north both have Saxon walling incorporating many Roman bricks. The blocked doorway high up on the south side is thought to have led to a west gallery. A north aisle was added c1190 with a two bay arcade of pointed arches with a round pier. The aisle has one small window of this period. The chancel was remodelled c1250 with renewed lancets and buttresses to support two bays of quadripartite rib-vaulting. There are traces of wall-paintings of that period showing the Adoration of the Lamb. The late 15th century chapel on the north side has the unusual feature of a fireplace. In a drastic restoration in 1866 Ford & Hesketh extended the nave one more bay to the west, provided a new south porch, built a small NW tower west of the aisle and added chambers at the SE corner of the nave and north of the aisle. They also replaced the chancel arch, north of which is an altar recess with a 13th century piscina.

The pulpit given by Sir Francis Vincent in 1620 retains an hour glass. The altar rail is of c1630. There is a fine 13th century oak chest. Several windows contain 15th century stained glass from Costessey Hall, Norfolk, and there is also some 16th century continental glass. The church has two of the earliest and best brasses in England, those of Sir John d'Abernon, d1277, the only brass of a knight with a lance, and Sir John d'Abernon, d1327. There are other brasses of Anne Norbury, d1464, the baby Elyn Bray, d1516, shown in swaddling clothes, Thomas Lyfelde and his wife Jane, d1592, with their daughter Jane, and John Prowd, d1497, the last a replica, the original being lost. There are recumbent effigies of Sir Thomas Vincent, d1613, and his wife, and there is a kneeling figure of 1633 showing Sir John Norbury in replacement of an older monument of c1500.

SUNBURY   *St Mary*   TQ 106686

The nave and west tower are of 1752, but in 1856 Teulon drastically remodelled the church and added a chancel.

Tatsfield Church

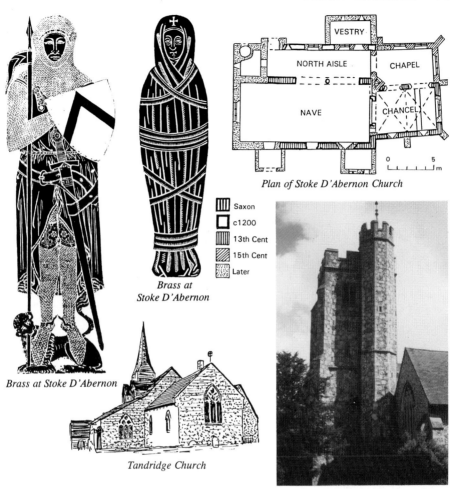

Plan of Stoke D'Abernon Church

IIII Saxon

□ c1200

III 13th Cent

▨ 15th Cent

▦ Later

*Brass at
Stoke D'Abernon*

Brass at Stoke D'Abernon

Tandridge Church

Tower at Stoke

TANDRIDGE   *St Peter*   TQ 375512

The chancel has one Norman north window and beside it is a Norman doorway, unusual since priest's doorways of that period are almost always on the south side. The chancel was partly rebuilt in the early 14th century and both it and the nave have trussed rafter roofs of that period. Four cross-braced posts at the west end support a bell-turret with a shingled spire. The south aisle was added in 1844 and the still wider north aisle was added in 1874 by Sir George Gilbert Scott.

TATSFIELD   *St Mary*   TQ 417562

In 1838 a vestry and a porch with a tower above were inserted into the west end of a Norman nave with two small original windows on the north side. The chancel is also Norman but has on each side a 13th century lancet with fine internal mouldings. The east window is of c1300, and the nave south wall has one window of that period and another which is 15th century. There is a monument to John Corbett, d1711.

Thorpe Church　　　　　　　　　*Tower at Thames Ditton*

THAMES DITTON　*St Nicholas*　TQ 161674

From the east the church has four gables, the 13th century chancel being flanked on the south by a chapel added with a south aisle by Ferrey in 1864, and on the north by an early 16th century chapel, beyond which is a brick outer chapel of 1826. The chancel had one north lancet, below which is a brick four-centred arch to the chapel. The low west tower is early 13th century. The block-capital shaped Norman font has small heads at the corners and lunettes with motifs in medallions such as the Lamb and Cross and an animal falling onto its horns. There is a late medieval Easter Sepulchre with six shafts carrying a canopy. There are brasses of Robert Smythe, d1539, and his wife Katherine, William Notte, d1576, and his wife Elizabeth, d1587, Erasmus Forde, d1533, and his wife Julyan, d1559, John Polsted, d1540, and his wife Anne (made in 1582), Julian, d1586 and her two husbands John Boothe, d1548, and Cuthbert Blakeden, d1540, and John Cheke, d1590, and his wife Isabel, all of them with children. There is also a wall monument to Sidney Godolphin, d1732.

THORPE　*St Mary*　TQ 024687

There is a Norman chancel arch of two orders flanked by a pair of 15th century squints. The 13th century arcades were replaced in the 19th century and the rest has been much restored apart from the 17th century brick tower with diagonal west buttresses. In the chancel the ogee-headed sedilia, piscina and windows now blocked by an organ chamber are 14th century. The nave roof has tie-beams with king-posts and four-way struts. The font is probably 18th century. The altar rails are of c1700. There is a monument with a praying cherub to Elizabeth Townsend, d1754, and also brasses of John Bonde, d1578, and his wife Joan, and William Denham, d1593, and his wife Joan, both couples with many children.

THURSLEY   *St Michael*   SU 901394

In 1927 two double-splayed Saxon windows were discovered in the north wall of the chancel, which has a chancel arch and two south lancets of the 13th century. One Norman window survives on the north side of the nave. Otherwise the exterior dates mostly from the restoration of 1860 by Ferrey and additions made by Penfold in 1883-6 which has given the church a western baptistry into which leads the porch, a north aisle and a south transeptal vestry. Over the middle bay of the nave is a mid 15th century wooden cage on four posts supporting a bell-turret. There are royal arms of George III dated 1783. The font bowl with ring moulding and a band of chevrons may be 11th century. The chest is of 1622. There is a monument to Katharine Woods, d1793.

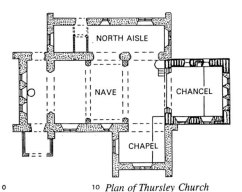

Plan of Thursley Church

Chancel at Thursley

Saxon
13th Century
14th Century
15th Century
Later & Modern

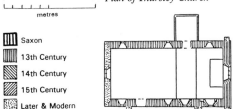

Plan of Wanborough Church

Thursley Church

TITSEY   *St James*   TQ 409550

A brass to William Gresham, d1579, with his wife Beatrice, and a monument of 1660 to Sir John Gresham, d1643, plus a foliated 13th century cross-slab, lie in the church of 1861 by J.L.Pearson with a south tower with a shingled broach-spire.

WALTON-ON-THAMES   *St Mary*   TQ 102665

The north arcade has Norman circular piers with scalloped capitals now carrying 14th century arches matching the south arcade, above which is a 16th century brick clerestory. The nave roof and upper parts of the aisle are of c1630. The north aisle windows are late medieval. The set-offs of the buttresses of the 15th century west tower were smoothed out in the 19th century. The organ case dates from c1700. There is a huge monument by Roubiliac to Richard Boyle, Viscount Shannon, d1740, who is depicted leaning against a gun. There is also a seated figure of his daughter. The brass of John Selwyn, Keeper of Oatlands Park, d1587, and his wife Susan, also has a scene showing a man riding a stag in memory of John's feat of jumping onto a stag, riding it up to Queen Elizabeth and stabbing it to death at her feet. There is a replica of a stolen scold's bridle of 1633.

WALTON-ON-THE-HILL   *St Peter*   TQ 224551

The 15th century chancel is heavily restored but retains original sedilia and piscina. Under recess outside is a worn effigy of the priest John de Walton, d1268. The nave and tower are of 1818 by Daniel Alexander. A north aisle was added in 1870 and in 1895 the present tower top replaced the original, which was octagonal with large turrets. There is a lead font bowl of the 1150s which originally had twelve figures of the Apostles, although only eight now survive. The SE window of the nave contains 17th century foreign glass.

Walton-on-Thames Church

Brass at
Walton-on-Thames

Chancel at Walton-on-the-Hill

Walton-on-Thames Church

Font at Walton-on-the-Hill

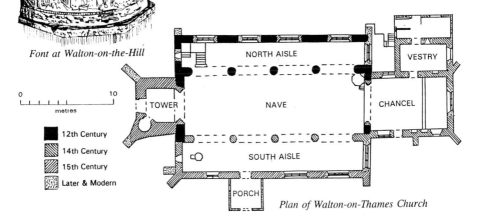

Plan of Walton-on-Thames Church

WANBOROUGH *St Bartholomew* SU 935489

This is a small 13th century single chamber with three lancets on the north side and two plus a doorway on the south. The SE window is 14th century and the east window is 15th century. The roof with a moulded longitudinal beam connecting collar-beams was much restored in 1862, after the chapel had been unused for a long time. Parts of the screen are medieval.

Wanborough Church

WARLINGHAM   *All Saints*   TQ 356590

Until lengthened and given a south aisle in the late 19th century this was a 13th century single chamber with three original doorway and only lancets (some restored) except for the renewed east window of c1340. There are double sets of sedilia and piscina, those further west serving a rood screen altar. The octagonal font and the wall painting of St Christopher carrying Christ are 15th century.

West Horsley Church

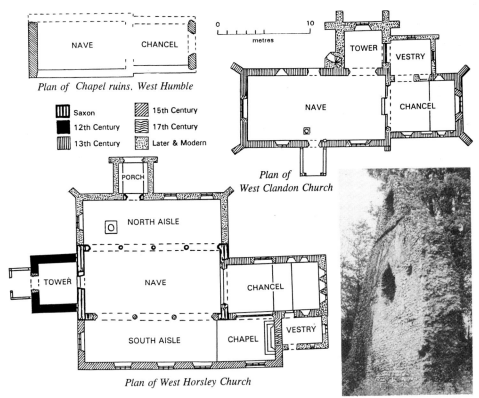

Plan of Chapel ruins, West Humble

▥	Saxon	▨	15th Century
■	12th Century	〰	17th Century
▦	13th Century	⣿	Later & Modern

Plan of West Clandon Church

Plan of West Horsley Church

Chapel ruins, West Humble

WEST CLANDON   *St Peter & St Paul*   TQ 044513

The nave and chancel are 13th century and there are traces of lancets flanking the renewed 14th century east window. In the nave SE corner is a pillar piscina of c1200. The three painted figures on a board must be from a former rood screen. The north tower was added in 1879, the spire being rebuilt in 1913. There are old pews and some 17th century medallions amongst the early 19th century glass. On the porch is a panel showing a dragon and a reptile in combat.

WEST HORSLEY   *St Mary*   TQ 088527

A west doorway of c1200 and a lancet above look into a slightly later tower. The east face of this wall has slight traces of wall paintings. The chancel arch is also of c1200 and has a blocked later half-arch north of it, whilst the north aisle doorway and arcade of roll-moulded arches is only slightly later. The aisle itself was rebuilt wider in 1869. The mid 13th century chancel has three east lancets and single lancets along the sides. Some of these contain stained glass medallions and there is a small kneeling figure of Sir James Berners, d1388. A 14th century panel on the south side depicts the Nativity. The south aisle and the screen are of c1500. The effigy of a 13th century priest is probably Ralph de Berners. There is a large tomb behind the organ to Sir Edward Nicholas, d1669, and there are monuments to Sir John Nicholas, d1704, and John Kendal, d1750.

WEST HUMBLE   *Dedication Unknown*   TQ 160519

All that remains of this chapel is the west wall of the nave and the lower part of the east wall of the narrower chancel.

WEST MOLESEY   *St Peter*   TQ 134684

e west tower with a higher stair turret and the octagonal font with quatrefoils are medieval. The yellow brick church is otherwise of 1843. The pulpit and tester are Jacobean.

WEYBRIDGE   *St James*   TQ 072648

J.L.Pearson's church of 1848 with an extra aisle added in 1864 contains several 18th and early 19th century tablets set high up under the tower, plus brasses of Thomas Inwood, d1586 and his three wives all kneeling, and John Woulde, d1598, and his wives Audry and Elizabeth, three children (Frances d1596, Dorothy, d1600, and Thomas, d1605) of Sir John and Dame Margaret Trevor, and three 15th century skeletons, presumably a man with two wives.

WIMBLEDON   *St Mary*   TQ 246715

The chancel was late medieval until mostly rebuilt by George Gilbert Scott in 1860. The nave was built by John Johnson in 1788, but replaced in 1843 by Scott and Moffatt. It has a west tower with a spire and there are three galleries. The Cecil Chapel of 1626-36 on the south side of the chancel contains a monument to Sir Edward Cecil, Viscount Wimbledon, d1638. The chapel has 17th century heraldic glass and there is also a 14th century figure of St George in one window.

WINDLESHAM   *St John the Baptist*   SU 931637

The south side has brickwork of 1680 after a fire, together with a porch and three reset medieval windows. The tower of that period was remodelled in 1838. A large new nave and north aisle and chancel of polychrome brick were added in 1874. In the original chancel is a tablet to Lieutenant-Colonel Robert Hemington, d1757.

Wisley Church

WISLEY   *Dedication Unknown*   TQ 057596

The nave and chancel are both Norman, the latter having two original windows (
each side. The east window is dated 1627 and of the same period are two-lig
windows on each side of the nave. Pointed-arched recesses of the 13th century (
into the jambs of a plain Norman chancel arch. The west windows and north doorv
are neo-Norman of 1872.

WITLEY   *All Saints*   SU 946397

The double-splayed windows on the
south side and high up in the west
gable suggest a Saxon date for the
nave, although the south doorway
looks Early Norman. On the south wall
are traces of wall-paintings showing the
life of the Virgin. At the end of the 12th
century the chancel was replaced by a
central tower with single-chamfered
arches into transepts and a new
chancel beyond. The south transept
retains two early lancets, whilst that in
the chancel south wall and two others
in the north chapel north wall, plus
another in the nave are late 13th
century. The arch between chapel and
chancel is 14th century. The tower top
seems to be a 17th century
remodelling. Campaigns of 1844 and
1890 saw the addition of a north aisle
of two bays with a vestry west of it,
the addition of the porch, the rebuilding
of the north transept and its extension
to the north to contain the organ. The
chancel was then remodelled inside but
retains an original piscina. The 13th
century octagonal font has a central
stem and eight shafts all merging into
one capital. There is a brass of
c1530 to Thomas Jonys, a
court official of Henry VIII, and
his wife Jane.

Witley Church

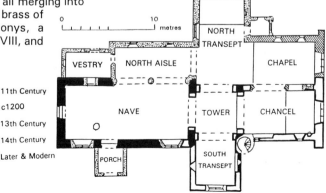

- ■ 11th Century
- □ c1200
- ▥ 13th Century
- ▧ 14th Century
- ▦ Later & Modern

Plan of Witley Church

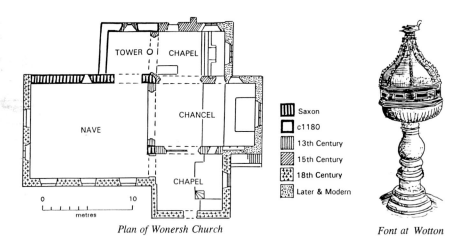

Plan of Wonersh Church   Font at Wotton

WONERSH   *St John the Baptist*   TQ 015451

In 1793 the nave and south aisle were rebuilt after a fire as one body of brick, although the north wall is still Saxon work with one small renewed window, and from it projects a north transeptal tower of the 1180s with a pointed arch to the nave and a top of 1751. The south chapel is also of 1793 but has a 13th century arch towards the chancel. The north chapel is 15th century and has a single arch towards the chancel. The east walls of both these parts were rebuilt in 1901 by Sir Charles Nicholson. There are Royal Arms of George III and several chandeliers, most of them copies of a set of the 1790s. The monuments include a 14th century tomb chest, an Elizabethan tablet, and brasses of Thomas Elyot, d1467, and his wife Alice, and Henry Elyot, d1503, and his wife Joan and twenty-three children.

Wonersh Church

Worpleston Church

WOODMANSTERNE   *St Peter*   TQ 277599

A medieval lancet survives in the NW corner of a nave of 1876-7 by Joseph Clarke to which E.F.Starling added a north aisle in 1960-1.

WORPLESTON   *St Mary*   SU 973536

The church lies alone above the village. An inscription on the west tower tells us that "Richard Exfold made XIV fote of yis touor". His will was proved in 1487 and another dated 1480 left money towards it. The tower has a NE stair turret, diagonal buttresses and a five-light west window over a doorway, and there are four-centred belfry lights. The cupola on the top was transferred from the rectory stables in 1766. The small clerestory windows of one or two lights with trefoiled heads and the aisles are 15th century but the large, plain mullioned windows must be 17th century and the arcades of double-hollow-chamfered arches on circular piers are late 13th century. Earlier 13th century work is the much restored north chapel with its two bay arcade to the chancel, but the two empty ogival-headed tomb recesses are 14th century. The late 17th century font and pulpit have been transferred here from Eton College. One north aisle window contains 14th century glass with figures under ogival canopies.

WOTTON   *St John*   TQ 126480

The 11th century tower has original plain arches to both east and west, proof that originally there was a nave to the west of it, footings of part of which can be seen. The tower has a two stage pyramidal roof like those of the Welsh Marches. In the 13th century the west arch was blocked up and provided with a lancet and a new nave and chancel were built to the east, whilst a doorway was provided on the south side of the tower. The north chapel and single bay north aisle are also 13th century and are divided by a 17th century screen. There is also a 17th century font with an ogival-shaped cover. The north chapel contains kneeling effigies of George Evelyn, d1603, and his two wives, and Richard Evelyn, d1634, and his wife, a bust of Elisabeth Darcy, d1634, plain coffin shaped slabs to John Evelyn, d1706, and his wife, d1709, and a tablet of 1778 by Robert Chambers to Sir John Evelyn. Beyond the chapel lies a late 17th century mausoleum in which many of the family lie buried.

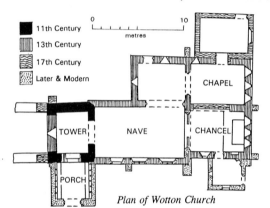

Plan of Wotton Church

Tablet at Wotton

Wotton Church

OTHER ANGLICAN CHURCHES IN SURREY

ADDLESTONE - St Paul - 1836 by James Savage. Brick. Lancets. West tower.
ASH - St Mark - 1847 by Woodyer. At Wyke.
ASHFORD - St Michael - 1928 by Sir Giles Gilbert Scott. Left unfinished.
ASHSTEAD - St George - 1905 by Sir Arthur Blomfield & Son. Brick.
BAGSHOT - St Anne - 1884 by Alec Cheer. South tower. Polychrome brick.
BARNES - St Michael - 1891-3 by Charles Innes.
BARNES - Holy Trinity - 1868 by Thomas Allom.
BLACKHEATH - St Martin - 1895 by C.Harrison Townsend.
BLINDLEY HEATH - St John Evangelist - 1842. Apsidal chancel & aisle 1886.
BOURNE - St Thomas - Lady Chapel 1862, rest 1911 by H.Sidebotham.
BROCKHAM - Christ Church - 1846 by Ferrey. Cruciform.
BROOKWOOD - St Saviour - 1909 by J.H.Ball.
BURGH HEATH - St Mary - 1909. Flint chequerwork exterior.
BURPHAM - St Luke - 1859 by Woodyer. Lancets, except east window.
BUSBRIDGE - St John st Baptist - 1865-7 by G.G.Scott
BYFLEET - St John Baptist - 1910-12 by W.D.Caroe.
CAMBERLEY - St Michael - 1849-51 by Woodyer. Tower & spire 1891.
CAMBERLEY - St Paul - 1902 by W.D.Caroe. Half timbered.
CARSHALTON - Good Shepherd - 1930 by Martin Travers & T.F.W.Grant.
CATERHAM - St John - 1881 by W.Bassett Smith.
CHEAM - St Philip - 1873-4 by Carpenter. Red Brick. Lancets.
CHELSHAM - St Christopher - 1907 by J.C.King. East end 1967.
CHURT - St John - 1868 by Ewan Christian.
CLAYGATE - Holy Trinity - 1840 by H.E.Kendall. Neo-Norman in grey brick.
COLDHARBOUR - Christ Church - 1848 by Ferrey in late 13th century style.
CROYDON - St Andrew - 1857 by Ferrey. Later additions.
CROYDON - St Augustine - 1881-4 by J.Oldrid Scott. Crossing tower.
CROYDON - Christ Church - 1851-2 by Teulon. Chancel added later.
CROYDON - Emanuel - 1899 by T.Roger Smith.
CROYDON - St James - 1827-9 by Robert Wallace. Chancel of 1881.
CROYDON - St Mary Magdalene - 1868-70 by E.Buckton Lamb. NE Tower later.
CROYDON - St Matthew - 1866 by A.W.Blomfield . Chancel added 1877.
CROYDON - St Michael - 1880-3 by J.L.Pearson. Unfinished south porch tower.
CROYDON - St Mildred - 1931-2 by C.G.Hare. At Addiscombe.
CROYDON - St Peter - 1849-51 by Sir G.G.Scott. West tower with spire.
DOCKENFIELD - Good Shepherd - 1910 by W.Curtis Green. Domestic looking.
DORMANSLAND - St John - 1883 by Sir Arthur Blomfield.
EAST MOLESEY - St Paul - 1854 by Salter & Laforest. Tower added 1888.
EAST SHEEN - Christ Church - 1862-4 by Sir Arthur Blomfield. North aisle 1887.
EGHAM HYTHE - St Paul - 1931-6 by John Coleridge. Crossing tower with spire.
ENGLEFIELD GREEN - St Simon & St Jude - 1859 by E.B.Lamb. Cruciform
EPSOM COMMON - Christ Church - 1876 by Sir Arthur Blomfield. NW tower.
ESHER GREEN - Christ Church - 1853-5 by Benjamin Ferrey.
FARNCOME - St John the Evangelist - 1847,1860,1875by Scott. Additions 1881.
FARNHAM - St James - 1876 by Woodyer.
FELBRIDGE - St John - 1865 by William White. Decorated style.
FRIMLEY - St Andrew - 1911 by H.R. & B.A.Poulter.
GRAFHAM - St Andrew - 1861-4 by Woodyer, who lived at the Grange nearby.
GUILDFORD - St Saviour - 1895 by H.S.Legg & Sons. Large NW tower.
GUILDFORD - Christ Church - 1868 by Ewan Christian.
HALE - St Mark - 1844 by Benjamin Ferrey. Round tower on south side.

HAM - St Andrew - 1830-1 by E.Lapidge. Aisle 1860. Chancel 1900-1.
HAMBLEDON - St Peter - Medieval foundation entirely rebuilt in 1846.
HASLEMERE - St Christopher - 1902 by Charles Spooner. North chapel 1935.
HASLEMERE - St Steplen - 1838. Enlarged by J.W.Penfold in 1876.
HATCHFORD - St Matthew - Nave 1850, chancel 1859 by Francis & Son.
HERSHAM - St Peter - 1887 by J.L.Pearson. NW tower with broach spire.
HINDHEAD - St Alban - 1907-10 by J.D.Coleridge. Not completed until 1931.
HOLMBURY ST MARY - St Mary - 1879 by G.W.Street. Contains older paintings.
HOOK - St Paul - 1881-3 by Carpenter & Ingelow. Single chamber. Dec style.
HURST GREEN - St John - 1912 by John Oldrid Scott. Extended 1962.
KINGSWOOD - St Andrew - 1848-52 by Ferrey. Copy of Shottesbrook Church, Berks.
LIMPSFIELD - St Andrew - 1895 by Sir Reginald Blomfield.
LONG CROSS - Christ Church - 1847 by Willoughby.
LOWER KINGSWOOD - St Sophia - 1891 by Sidney Barnsley. Byzantine capitals.
LOWFIELD HEATH - St Michael - 1867 by William Burges. West porch. South tower.
LYNE - Holy Trinity - 1849 by Francis. Cruciform.
MILFORD - St John - Undated. Morris glass. Webb family Mausoleum in churchyard.
MITCHAM - St Barnabas - 1914 by H.P.Burke-Downing. North aisle never built.
NEW MALDON - Christ Church - 1866 by Freshwater & Brandon.
NORBITON - St Peter - 1841 by Scott & Moffatt. NW tower. Yellow & white brick.
NORBURY - St Stephen - 1908 by W.S.Weatherley.
NORTH BEDDINGTON - All Saints - 1931 by H.P.Burke-Downing.
NORTH HOLMWOOD - St John 1875 by Rhode Hawkins. NW tower.
OTTERSHAW - Christchurch - 1864 by Sir Gilbert Scott.
OUTWOOD - St John the Baptist - 1869 by Burges. West tower 1876.
OXSHOTT - St Andrew - 1912 by Caroe & Passmore.
PEASLAKE - St Mary - 1889 by Ewan Christian.
PETERSHAM - All Saints - 1907-8 by John Kelly. Large, red brick. Romanesque.
PIXHAM - St Martin - 1903 by Lutyens. Nave also had a secular use.
PYRFORD - Good Shepherd - 1963-4 by David Nye. T-plan with steep roof.
RANMORE COMMON - St Bartholomew - 1859 by Sir George Gilbert Scott.
REDHILL - St John - Aisles 1867 but mostly 1889-95 by Pearson. Tall SW tower.
REDHILL - St Matthew - 1866 by Hahn.
REIGATE - St Mark - 1860 by Field & Hilton.
REIGATE - St Peter - 1955 by E.F.Starling. Elliptical hall & church combined.
RICHMOND - Christ Church - 1893 by Sir Arthur Bromfield.
RICHMOND - Holy Trinity - 1870 by R.Brandon. Addition 1880 by Luck.
RICHMOND - St John the Divine - 1831-6 by L.Vulliamy. Chancel 1905 by A.Grove.
RICHMOND - St Matthias - 1858 by Sir Giles Gilbert Scott. NW tower. Apse. Grand.
ST HELIER - Bishop Andrewe's - 1933 by Geddes Hyslop. Broad crossing tower.
ST HELIER - St Peter - 1932 by Sir Charles Nicholson.
SALFORDS - Christ the King - 1958-67 by David Nye.
SANDERSTEAD HILL - St Mary - 1926 by Greenaway and Newberry.
SELSDON - St John - 1935-6 by Newberry & Fowler. NE tower.
SHACKLEFORD - St Mary - 1865 by Sir George Gilbert Scott. Central tower. Apse.
SHAMLEY GREEN - Christ Church - 1864 by C.H.Howell. Decorated style.
SHIRLEY - St John - 1856 by Sir G.G.Scott. Tomb of Ruskin's parents in churchyard.
SIDLOW BRIDGE - Emmanuel - 1861 by Clutton.
SOUTH HOLMWOOD - St Mary Magdalene - Chancel 1838, nave 1842, tower 1863.
SOUTH NORWOOD - Holy Innocents - 1894-5 by Bodley.
STAINES - St Peter - 1893-4 by G.H.Fellowes Prynne.

STAINES - Christ Church - 1961-2 by H.Norman Haines. Square with central lantern.
SURBITON - Christ Church - 1862-3 by C.L.Luck. Lengthened 1866. Chapels later.
SURBITON - St Andrew - 1871 by Sir Arthur Blomfield. Yellow & red brick.
SURBITON - St Mark - 1845, remodelled 1855. Rebuilt after war damage 1960.
SURBITON - St Matthew - 1874-5 by C.L.Luck. Big and fine, SW tower with spire.
SUTTON - All Saints - 1863-6 by S.S.Teulon. Large. Big west tower.
SUTTON - Christ Church - 1888 by Newman & Jacques. Red brick. Polygonal apse.
SUTTON - St Barnabas - 1884-91 by Carpenter & Ingelow. Red brick.
SUTTON - St John Baptist - 1915 by Greenaway & Newberry.
SUTTON - St Nicholas - Rebuilt 1862-4 by Edwin Nash. Gibson mausoleum 1777.
THORNTON HEATH - St Alban - Nave 1889, chancel 1894, by Bucknall & Comper.
TILFORD - All Saints - 1867 by Ewan Christian.
TONGHAM - St Paul - 1865 by Ewan Christian. Detached brick tower.
UPPER NORWOOD - All Saints - 1827-9 by James Savage. Chancel 1861.
UPPER NORWOOD - St John Evangelist - 1878-87 by Pearson. Red brick.
UPPER SUNBURY - St Saviour - 1911-3 by J.S.Alder.
VIRGINIA WATER - Christ Church - 1839 by W.F.Pocock. Cruciform. Tower & spire.
WALLINGTON - Holy Trinity - 1867 by Habershon & Brock. Low apse. Tower & spire.
WESTCOTT - Holy Trinity - 1852 by Sir George Gilbert Scott. Shingled bell-turret.
WESTON GREEN - All Saints - 1939 by Sir Edward Maufe. NE bell tower.
WEYBRIDGE - St Michael - 1874 by Butterfield. Polychrome brick.
WIMBLEDON - All Saints - 1891-3 by Micklethwaite & Somers Clarke.
WIMBLEDON - Christ Church - 1859-60 by S.S.Teulon. Enlarged 1881.
WIMBLEDON - St John - 1875 by T.G.Jackson. Red brick. Decorated style
WIMBLEDON - St Mark - 1968-9 by Humphreys & Hurst. Pentagonal plan.
WIMBLEDON - St Matthew - c1910 by E.C.Shearman. Rebuilt after WWII.
WIMBLEDON - St Paul - 1877 by Micklethwaite & Somers Clarke. Brick. Fleche. Dec.
WINDLESHAM - St Saviour - 1867 by Bodley. Brick. Shingled belfry.
WOKING - Christ Church - 1889 by W.F.Unsworth. Large, brick, lancets.
WOKING - St Mary of Bethany - 1907 by Caroe. Brick. Voussoirs of thin tiles.
WOKING - St John - 1842 by G.G.Scott but much enlarged later.
WOLDINGHAM - St Agatha - 1832. Tiny single chamber of flint.
WOLDINGHAM - St Paul - 1933 by Sir Herbert Baker. Flushwork inscription on tower.
WOODHAM - All Saints - 1893 by W.F.Unsworth. Tile-hung crossing.
WOODSIDE - St Luke - 1870 by W.V.Arnold. East end rebuilt 1949.
WORCESTER PARK - St Mary - 1895 by A.Thomas. Polygonal apse. Fleche. Flint.
WRECCLESHAM - St Peter - 1840 by James Harding. Enlarged 1862 and 1877.

FURTHER READING

The Victoria County History of Surrey (several volumes, various dates)
The Buildings of England, Surrey volume, Ian Nairn & Nicholaus Pevsner, 1962
A List of Monumental Brasses in Surrey, Mill Stephenson, 1921
Surrey Archeological Collections (published annually)

GLOSSARY OF ARCHITECTURAL TERMS

Abacus	- A flat slab on top of a capital.
Apse	- Semi-circular or polygonal east end of a church containing an altar.
Ashlar	- Masonry of blocks with even faces and square edges.
Baroque	- A whimsical and odd form of the Classical architectural style.
Beakhead	- Decorative motif of bird or beast heads, often biting a roll moulding.
Broaches	- Sloping half pyramids adapting an octagonal spire to a square tower.
Cartouche	- A tablet with an ornate frame, usually enclosing an inscription.
Chancel	- The eastern part of a church used by the clergy.
Chevron Ornament	- A Norman ornament with continuous Vs forming a zig-zag.
Clerestory	- An upper storey pierced by windows lighting the floor below.
Collar Beam	- A tie-beam used higher up near the apex of the roof.
Crossing Tower	- A tower built on four arches in the middle of a cruciform church.
Cruciform Church	- A cross-shaped church with transepts forming the arms of the cross.
Cusp	- A projecting point between the foils of a foiled Gothic arch.
Dado	- The decorative covering of the lower part of a wall or screen.
Decorated	- The architecture style in vogue in England c1300-1380.
Dog Tooth	- Four-cornered stars placed diagonally and raised pyramidally.
Easter Sepulchre	- A recess in a chancel which received an effigy of Christ at Easter.
Elizabethan	- Of the time of Queen Elizabeth I (1558-1603).
Fan Vault	- Vault with fan-like patterns. In fashion from c1440 to 1530.
Foil	- A lobe formed by the cusping of a circle or arch.
Four Centred Arch	- A low, flattish arch with each curve drawn from two compass points.
Gargoyle	- A water spout shaped like an animal or human head below a parapet.
Head Stops	- Heads of humans or beasts forming the ends of a hoodmould.
Herringbone Masonry	- Courses of stones alternately sloping at 45 degrees to horizontal.
Hoodmould	- A projecting moulding above a lintel or arch to throw off water.
Jacobean	- Of the time of King James I (1603-25).
Jamb	- The side of a doorway, window, or other opening.
King-post	- A post connecting a tie-beam or collar-beam with the roof ridge beam.
Lancet	- A long and comparatively narrow window with a pointed head.
Light	- A compartment of a window.
Lintel	- A horizontal stone or beam spanning an opening.
Merlon	- An upstanding part of a crenellated parapet. The indents are crenels.
Miserichord	- Bracket underneath hinged choir stall seat to support standing person.
Mullion	- A vertical member dividing the lights of a window.
Nave	- The part of a church in which the congregation sits or stands.
Nook-shaft	- A column set in the angle of a pier or respond or jamb of an opening.
Norman	- A division of English Romanesque architecture from 1066 to 1200.
Ogival Arch	- Arch of oriental origin with both convex and concave curves.
Pediment	- Low-pitched gable used in classical and neo-classical architecture.
Perpendicular	- The architectural style in vogue in England c1380-1540.
Pilaster	- Flat buttress or pier attached to a wall.
Piscina	- A stone basin used for rinsing out holy vessels after a mass.
Plinth	- The projecting base of a wall.
Queen-posts	- Two vertical struts placed symmetrically on a tie-beam or collar-beam.
Quoins	- Dressed stones at the corners of a building.
Rere-Arch	- An arch on the inside face of a window embrasure or doorway.
Reredos	- Structure behind and above an altar forming a backdrop to it.
Respond	- A half pier or column bonded into a wall and carrying an arch.
Reticulation	- Tracery with a net-like appearence. Current c1330-70.
Rood Screen	- A screen with a crucifix mounted on it between a nave and chancel.
Sedilia	- Seats for clergy (usually three) in the south wall of a chancel.
Spandrel	- The surface between two arches or between an arch and a corner.
Squint	- Opening allowing the main altar to be seen from a subsiderary one.
Tester	- A sounding board above a 17th or 18th century pulpit.
Tie-Beam	- A beam connecting the slopes of a roof at or near its foot.
Tracery	- Intersecting ribwork in the upper part of a later Gothic window.
Transom	- A horizontal member dividing the lights of a window.
Tympanum	- The space between the lintel of a doorway and the arch above it.
Venetian Window	- Window with square headed lights on either side of an arched light.
Victorian	- Of the time of Queen Victoria (1837-1901).
Voussoir	- A wedge shaped stone forming part of an arch.